Shops and Showrooms

An International Survey

Karl Kaspar

Shops and Showrooms

An International Survey

Frederick A. Praeger, Publishers
New York · Washington

BOOKS THAT MATTER

Published in the United States of America in 1967
by Frederick A. Praeger, Inc., Publishers
111 Fourth Avenue, New York, N. Y. 10003
All rights reserved
Copyright in Stuttgart in 1967 by Verlag Gerd Hatje, Stuttgart, Germany
Library of Congress Catalog Card Number: 67–20402
Printed in Germany

Translated from the German by Lieselotte Mickel

Contents · Inhalt

The search for new techniques in the age-old endeavour to bring goods for sale to man's notice is unceasing. Psychologists, sociologists, economists and management consultants are brought in to reduce the risk of faulty planning to a minimum. They assemble all the factors that affect the sales and lay-out of a shop, make surveys of the size and social structure of the market, analyze the purchasing power and consumer habits of the district and study the shop's commercial status and its position in relation to its competitors. The best possible organizational methods within the shop are examined, such as the most effective means of directing the customers' movements, the most favourable siting of personnel and goods, and the most logical lay-out of sales and stock rooms.

A remarkable degree of accuracy has now been reached in the technique of assessing all these factors, and their application suggests that they have already had far-reaching results. They have promoted a strongly marked differentiation between various types of shop and, since the 'fifties, have brought into being completely new forms of trade – the self-service supermarket, the discount house, the drive-in shop, and the mobile shop. In addition they have contributed, particularly in the food trade, to the fact that more and more independent, individual traders have merged into companies or joined up as chain stores. Even businessmen whose firms have affiliated branches are constantly striving to strengthen the links between them. They all stand in stiff competition for trade, both amongst themselves and against the department stores. Generally, they are far more intent on achieving the maximum results of rationalization, at least in the present stage of development, than on any achievement in the field of interior design.

The system of marketing and selling has, as a result, had a profound influence on shop design. Free choice and self-service at their various different levels (from the advisory personnel in attendance to the fully automatic sales lay-out) bring about a decisive transformation of interior design. In the past the goods were brought to the customer; now the customer is led to the goods. The human contact between buyer and seller is giving way to the visual appeal arising from the sophisticated wrappings of the goods and their effective presentation. The presentation can become such a dominating factor that the architectural framework recedes completely into the background to become an anonymous shell; and since the carriers of the goods – the shelves, trolleys or refrigerated display cabinets – are largely mass-produced objects there is often very little noticeable difference between one self-service store and another (Ill. 1). The technical perfection of 'mass merchandising' has had the drawback of producing an extensive uniformity in shop design which restricts the scope of the architect considerably.

Individual solutions in which the architectural quality is above average are to be found largely amongst the specialty shops. Here the size of the shop is far less of a determining factor than the concern to hit an unmistakably individual note. The illustrated section of this volume contains a large number of examples demonstrating how, in spite of extremely limited space, a handsome and impressive effect has been achieved. The specialty shop offering a specific range of goods still relies on the endeavour to satisfy each customer's wish in a personal way. Individual service, expert advice, and the performance of additional service are intended to tie the consumer to the venture as a regular customer. The design of the shop plays an important role in this emotional process, since it establishes the shop's atmosphere and affects its image. It can induce certain moods: gaiety and extravagance in the fashion boutique, relaxed informality in the teenager shop, solid elegance in the shoe shop or a precise objectivity in the camera shop. The architecture becomes emotionally charged and the choice of materials, lighting, colour and form makes an important contribution to setting the scene for the merchandise. The shell is by no means a characterless utilization of available space, noticed only by chance, but serves positively as the setting for the current display programme. Here the only limits set to the interior designer's creative imagination occur at the point where the architectural shell becomes an end in itself, an attraction as such. The I. Miller shoe-shop in New York (Ill. 2) with all its originality, clearly shows the problematic nature of such over-sophistication. Its columns, floors on different levels and the ceiling, which is over ten metres high in the centre of the room, are closely covered with scale-like, pliant wooden lasts, reminiscent of the buttresses and fan faulting of churches of the Middle Ages; this is a cathedral of retail business in which the sale of shoes is celebrated.

The business showroom, which forms the second group of examples, shows even more distinctly than the specialist shop the tendency to connect the way the product is presented with the image of the business. As a design project the showroom gives the architect even greater scope. The concern of the organization to demonstrate their progressiveness and receptivity by the originality of their showroom design helps a number of avant-garde projects to realization. In addition, the designer of such a showroom can usually rely on a generous budget. On the technical side, his planning is made easier by the fact that he does not have to house a complete range of goods with the necessary

1. Architecture as a neutral shell: shopping 'streets' in a self-service supermarket.

1. Architektur als neutrales Gehäuse: Einkaufs-»Straßen« in einem Selbstbedienungs-Supermarkt.

stock and storage space this entails, but only a comparatively small number of display and demonstration models. Large, well-known organizations can even allow themselves to treat the exhibited articles as incidental, and concentrate on emphasizing the spatial treatment of the showroom. The Olivetti branch in Venice (Ill. 3 and 4) is an example. In the almost empty ground floor which is given its distinctive character by the use of rich materials, marble walls, and a floor of glass mosaics, two accents dominate whose only connections to the product are by association: a metal sculpture with mirroring arches and a staircase made from polished concrete blocks which forms a kind of counterpoint. A solution of this kind, relying on the knowledge of an assured market, offers the passer-by little concrete information on the product, but concentrates primarily on suggested prestige values: elegance, precision and exclusiveness. Abroad, Olivetti balances the mixture of information on the product and representation of their image more strongly in favour of the product. The exhibition rooms in Barcelona (p. 66) or Paris (p. 63) give some idea of this, together with the New York showroom with its highly sophisticated design. These Olivetti establishments demonstrate the possibility of giving each branch a distinct, individual character, and for this they call in the most eminent Italian architects. The porcelain factory of Rosenthal is an example of the opposite method. They have decorated their showrooms (Ill. 6 and p. 100) by treating them like a proprietary article, giving each one the same characteristic stamp. Whether in Paris, Zurich, or Berlin they differ only in nuances, behind which the constant factor of the uniform image of the firm remains clearly in evidence.

Although the showroom emphasizes the image-making aspect of the specialized business, in the third group of examples selected for this volume the emphasis is more on the service. A hairdresser's or a beauty salon, a travel agency or the ticket office of an airline company, are all service industries who sell their customers advice and assistance. The rooms in which the visitor is received are intended to awaken his interest, to heighten his expectations, to make him sympathetic to what is to be offered him. The setting of the offer becomes as important as the service itself. If the accents are placed correctly then this setting can spark off a whole gamut of positive reactions in the customer's subconscious: the corroboration of his social exclusiveness, the delight in belonging, the satisfaction of being able to afford something, or simply the plain pleasure of being attended by experts in pleasant surroundings. These are all feelings which encourage the desire to spend money. Our examples, such as the hairdressing salons illustrated on pp. 142 and 148 clearly show how the most varied methods can lead to this end. The cool objective mood of a ladies' hairdressing salon in London's West End which specializes in secretaries and models, appeals to its particular customers just as accurately as the Italian hairdressing salons where individual cubicles give the client the impression of being accorded special privileges. Both examples are typical of the concern to offer the customer an independent, unmistakable ambience, an atmosphere quite distinct from that of the average run of the mill hairdresser's.

This task is easiest for the agencies of tourist organizations, airlines that solicit custom for a specific country, or a national airline company. They can build on the attractiveness of a design coloured by aspects of folklore. However, the colour poster and the metre-square photograph alone are no more adequate as an answer than setting some antique chosen at random on the reception counter. Even a collection of accessories of this kind will not provide an effective solution. This can only be achieved when the various elements have been successfully integrated into the total design. A 'total design' of this kind is illustrated, for example, in the establishment of the Israel Airlines (Ill. 7 and p. 161) where a translucent cube in front of the facade lights up various combinations of the airline company's name, EL AL, in Hebrew and Latin characters. The rustic character of the surfaces,

2. Architecture as the dominant feature: a 'cathedral' of retail business. (I. Miller shoe shop, New York; architect: Victor Lundy).

2. Architektur als Dominante: eine »Kathedrale« des Einzelhandels (Schuhhaus I. Miller, New York; Architekt: Victor Lundy).

3, 4. Showroom of a very well-known business enterprise: products are not on display but represented symbolically (Olivetti branch, Venice; architect: Carlo Scarpa).

3, 4. Ausstellungsraum eines Unternehmens mit hohem Bekanntheitsgrad: statt Produktschau Repräsentation mit Symbolformen (Olivetti-Filiale, Venedig; Architekt: Carlo Scarpa).

5. Business showroom given an individual, unmistakable treatment: marble pedestals serve as display-stands, lamps of Murano glass, mural relief by C. Nivola (Olivetti branch, New York; architects: Studio BBPR).

5. Der Firmen-Ausstellungsraum als einmalige, unverwechselbare Lösung: Marmorsockel als Exponatträger, Lampen aus Muranoglas, Wandrelief von C. Nivola (Olivetti-Filiale, New York; Architekten: Studio BBPR).

the paved floor and rough textured walls, awakens subtle associations with the landscape and culture of Israel, as do the cacti and the breast-plate of a Jewish high priest which has been enlarged to form a wall sculpture. The ceiling of stylized aeroplanes indicates the specific purpose of the rooms without disrupting its formal unity.

Where it is not a question simply of catering for a real need, as with the food supermarket, or of satisfying an already established consumer demand, then there lies at the source of all selling the need to transform the indifferent attitude of a passer-by into one of increasing interest, finally of bringing him to the point where he enters the shop as a potential customer. In this process the eye plays the primary role. Shop design begins, then, with bringing the merchandise to the eye of the passer-by in the most attractive and comprehensive way possible – a function which the shop window, the show case or even the whole facade of the shop can take over if it is glazed to its full width and to a sufficient height, thereby making the whole of the interior into a single shop window. With this aim of opening outwards, German and Swiss shop designers, for instance, compete so extravagantly on these lines that some experts are beginning to find this vast uniformity monotonous. Anodised aluminium is used just as commonly as glass; shop windows reach down to the pavement, there are plate glass doors, glass cases, windows wholly of glass; and there is still no end in sight of this trend. Famous specialist shops can afford understatement in their display. However, the renunciation of direct soliciting for the merchandise presupposes an unusually high degree of familiarity with the product offered and the reputation of the firm. In the candle shop in Vienna (Ill. 8 and p. 94) which has become widely known, the architect applied this idea when he let the customary show windows shrink into two diagonally set panes no larger than the average fluorescent lighting panel. In return he gave the aluminium-covered facade of the shop such a distinctive form that the intensity of its visual appeal outrivals any 'standard' solution.

On the whole, however people adhere to the proven rule, and design for as large an area shop window as possible to give the widest possible over-all view of the actual goods offered. Where the narrow frontage of a building sets limits that are too restricted, additional window space is often gained by recessing the entrance area. Narrow-fronted buildings leave no alternative even when it means sacrificing valuable shop space. The recessed window bay also has the advantage of detaching the spectator from the stream of passers-by. He can slow down his step without being a nuisance to other pedestrians. This results in comparatively long pauses in front of the shop window and provides a better chance of the desire to buy coming to fruition. Psychologists discovered that this kind of bay must not be deeper than its width if it is to avoid creating subconscious feelings of constriction or even fear. They also urge that the bay should be splayed so as to form a funnel shape or that the walls be stepped back since sharp corners or a frontal "barricade" could provoke one to flight. They suggest also that the shop entrance should be assymmetrically placed at the inmost point of the bay. Symmetry apparently demands a conscious decision and this would reduce the subconsciously growing tendency to buy. Taking these considerations into account the architect Eduard Schrag has produced an ideal scheme (Ill. 9) in which island-shaped windows become an additional aid to directing the movements of the customer.

In this connection, a particularly interesting solution is offered by the system of mobile display windows which was developed for the Duesseldorf branch of Rosenthal (p. 100). A network of tracks recessed into the ceiling allows quick and easy changes to the standardized window and showcase panels as well as the wall-panels and glass doors, making it possible to completely alter the design of

6. Stylistic unity of shop design in all the Rosenthal Studio-Houses (Cologne Studio-House).

6. Stilistische Einheitlichkeit der Ladengestaltung bei allen Rosenthal-Studiohäusern (Studiohaus Köln).

the display window and entrance area overnight. By this method the length of the display window can be increased to more than five times the width of the frontage. The only restriction underlying this exceptionally flexible system is that the tracking system does not allow for other than angles of 90°; but for the comparatively small module of 70×70 centimetres this is hardly important.

The second stage in the process of soliciting the customer takes place inside the shop. Here not only visual information, but also sales talk, the personal contact between seller and potential buyer plays its part, and as an important final incentive, direct contact with the merchandise.

The extent to which the sales assistants play an active role here has, in its turn, considerable bearing on the interior design, even in the case of the specialty shop. The luxury variety, which conceals all but a few representative goods in cupboards and drawers, is the extreme case in point. This technique of selling is based on the assumption of a clientele able to formulate its wishes precisely and with a fairly accurate idea of what is available. It also demands well-trained sales assistants with sufficient flair to assess the customer's needs quickly and present goods that seem relevant. The salesman's expertise governs whether the first selection offered is correct, and herein lies the possible weakness of this system. However, its undeniable advantage is that it enhances the psychological value of the goods for sale. An individual piece of merchandise set in the foreground can suggest to the customer that the selection he is offered is precisely suited to his individual requirements. In haute couture, most of the selling is based on this method. From the point of view of interior design, it demands built-in cupboards, drawers, cabinets and counters, designed in such impressive materials and colours that the rest of the interior inevitably pales beside them (Ill. 10).

At the other extreme there is the specialty shop which spreads its goods in front of the customer as generously as possible. The Carnaby Street type fashion shop in London provides an example of this (Ill. 11). The unconventional, free and easy fairground atmosphere that prevails here is also carried into the interior design. Improvised stands or standard rails serve as racks for clothes; and an old chair or some other piece from the junk room, transformed into a pop-art object, is used to display the goods. Walls and ceilings are painted in strong or even strident colours and absurdly irrelevant objects used as decorative accessories compete in importance with the fashions on display.

The advocates of the 'standard solution' avoid both these extremes. Their credo calls for flexibility above all. Flexibility to allow for changing displays of current fashions and, in the long run, to enable them to cope with such eventualities as enlarging the range of goods or regrouping them. Their ideal is easily moveable furniture, interchangeable standardized units, neutral colours and evenly distributed ceiling lighting. All too often, the results are dull and characterless. In our selection we have chosen, therefore, examples in which flexibility was not achieved at the price of a dreary uniformity. Above all we have concentrated on solutions in which the firms have tried to give their premises an unmistakable personal stamp. It is true that often this was only possible at the cost of not being able to vary the interior. However, leading market researchers and trade experts now feel that the interior design of shops should be renewed at considerably shorter intervals than formerly to keep pace with developments in retail business. They suggest that, instead of modifying the initial basic design by giving too much consideration to possible future changes, it is more sensible to accept the existing features of the building and to allow for more frequent variations of the interior.

However, conversions are already an important feature of shop building. There is a particularly high percentage of modernization amongst the specialty shops that do not want to give up their ancient privileged position in the city. One would have thought that the predetermined size and shape of these

7. Successful formal association of 'flying' with 'Israel' (Office of the Israel Airlines, Frankfurt am Main; architects: Fautz and Rau).

7. Formal gelungene Assoziation zu »Fliegen« und »Israel« (Büro der Israel Airlines, Frankfurt am Main; Architekten: Fautz und Rau).

premises would be a considerable disadvantage; but, as the illustrated section shows, such restrictions have served to stimulate the designers to some of the most imaginative designs included. In nearly every case, the main difficulties to overcome shortage of space and useful working area, and the complications arising from awkward proportions, useless corners and inconveniently placed structural elements. In addition to the more usual means of adapting the interior, such as dropped ceilings, different wall colours and finishes, or contrasts in height and lighting to define special areas, they have used a number of imaginative devices to make a shop appear larger by disguising or apparently removing its boundaries. These devices range from perspective illusion (p. 33) to the Chinese puzzle effect achieved with curved or hexagonal forms (pp. 142 and 60) which deliberately obscure the original rectangular shape of the room. A few examples in which mirror walls create the optical illusion deserve particular mention. There is the candle shop in Vienna (Ill. 12 and p. 94) in which reflections in the narrow side panels create the illusion of a cross axis stretching to infinity as the customers walk past. Then there is the fashion shop in Genoa (Ill. 13 and p. 16), where mirrors and arches are so cunningly placed and interrelated that it becomes difficult to distinguish illusion from reality.

Effects such as these can be considerably heightened by clever lighting. There is a widespread theory that lighting is best where it is least in evidence. However, if one studies the examples in this volume in this connexion, one is tempted to take the opposite stand. Wherever rich, imaginative ideas and a specific atmosphere predominate, the forms of lighting used emphasize these accents. For instance, bowl lamps on wall brackets add a touch of 'Belle Epoque' to the laundry shop (Ill. 14), heavy studio spotlights on the ceiling of a camera shop recall a film studio (Ill. 15), and ceiling panels of illuminated prisms (Ill. 16) and cubes (Ill. 17) are immediately eyecatching. Of course such lighting effects do not make it possible to dispense with general background lighting or adjustable spotlights which can focus attention on a special piece of merchandise. However nowadays, the rules governing the appropriate strength and colour of light seldom pose design problems. The industry has plenty of well-tried solutions ready at hand to provide really adequate, yet lively, lighting- and spare the public unnaturally pallid faces.

The examples here have been grouped according to the simplest and most useful principle: arrangement by class of shop. This means that stylistically similar examples are often far apart and that national characteristics are not as easy to trace as in an arrangement by countries. On the other hand, this order offers the possibility of immediate comparison between related projects. For instance, if one takes the group of camera shops, in spite of any variations in size, shape, and layout of the showrooms, it becomes evident how carefully the designers set out to avoid confusion and overcrowding by bringing together the small unit of one camera into larger, eye-catching complexes, such as glass domes or glass counters. Or again, in the furniture shops, the designers have all tried to create, from elements that were as simple and flexible as possible, spatial effects which could serve as a neutral background for individual groupings and to isolate them from each other, without disrupting the continuity of the total display area.

But order according to classes of shop must not be taken too literally. A shop for sewing machines is quite certainly related to a showroom for electric typewriters or for apparatus for reading microfilms. In all three cases, the product must be individually displayed but at the same time its method of use must be demonstrated; this almost necessarily entails the division of the space into showroom and demonstration area. A music shop that keeps thousands of sheets of music, pocket scores and textbooks available, poses functional problems similar to a travel agency, in which a great number of prospectuses and catalogues must be readily at hand.

Both architect and businessman should find it rewarding to trace such interrelationships, to discover analogies over and above the narrow categorization into classes, and to apply them to future schemes of their own.

8. Instead of display windows and comprehensive display of goods, the arresting design of the shopfront promotes sales (see p. 94).

8. Verzicht auf Schaufenster mit umfassendem Warenangebot, statt dessen hoher Werbewert der expressiv gestalteten Ladenfront (siehe Seite 94).

Die Gegenwart sucht unermüdlich neue Wege für das uralte Bemühen, eine Ware an den Mann zu bringen. Psychologen, Soziologen, Betriebsökonomen und Rationalisierungsfachleute werden aufgeboten, um dabei das Risiko einer Fehlplanung auf ein Minimum zu beschränken. Sie tragen alle Faktoren zusammen, die das Verkaufs- und Raumprogramm eines Ladens beeinflussen: statistische Erhebungen über die Größe und die soziologische Struktur des Einzugsgebietes, Analysen über die Kaufkraft seiner Bewohner und ihre Konsumgewohnheiten, Studien über Verkehrslage und Konkurrenzsituation, verbunden mit Untersuchungen über die bestmögliche innerbetriebliche Organisation (zum Beispiel die optimale Wegführung im Kundenbereich, die günstigsten Personal- und Warenbewegungen oder die rationellste Aufteilung in Verkaufs- und Lagerräume).

Die Methoden, alle diese Faktoren zu erfassen, haben inzwischen einen beachtlichen Genauigkeitsgrad erreicht. In der Praxis legten sie weitreichende Konsequenzen nahe: Sie förderten die starke Differenzierung der Ladentypen und ließen seit den fünfziger Jahren ganz neue Betriebsformen entstehen – vom Selbstbedienungs-Supermarkt über das Discounthaus bis zum Drive-in-Laden und zum Shopmobile. Sie trugen, vor allem im Lebensmittelhandel, dazu bei, daß sich immer mehr selbständige Einzelhändler in Genossenschaften und Handelsketten zusammenschlossen. Auch die Unternehmer mit firmeneigenen Filialen sind ständig bemüht, ihr Netz noch dichter zu knüpfen. Sie alle stehen in hartem Wettbewerb untereinander und gegen die Warenhäuser. Von Ausnahmen abgesehen ist bei ihnen, wenigstens auf der gegenwärtigen Entwicklungsstufe, das Streben nach dem maximalen Rationalisierungseffekt weitaus größer als formale Ambitionen bei der Einrichtung.

Das System des Anbietens und Verkaufens hat demnach einen tiefgreifenden Einfluß auf die Ladengestaltung. Freiwahl und Selbstbedienung in ihren verschiedenen Stufen (vom bereitstehenden Beratungspersonal bis zur vollautomatischen Verkaufsanlage) bewirken einen einschneidenden Wandel der Einrichtung. Wurde bisher die Ware zum Kunden gebracht, so führt man nun den Kunden an die Ware heran. Der menschliche Kontakt zwischen Käufer und Verkäufer wird durch den optischen Appell ersetzt, der von dem raffiniert verpackten und übersichtlich präsentierten Warensortiment ausgeht. Seine Zurschaustellung kann so stark dominieren, daß der architektonische Rahmen dahinter völlig zurücktritt (Abb. 1). Er wird zum anonymen Gehäuse, und da auch die Warenträger – also die Regale, die Verkaufsgondeln oder Kühltruhen – überwiegend aus der industriellen Serienproduktion stammen, sind bei vielen Selbstbedienungsläden Unterschiede kaum mehr wahrnehmbar. Die technische Perfektion des »mass-merchandising« zeigt als Kehrseite eine weitgehende Uniformität der Ladengestaltung und setzt damit dem Architekten enge Grenzen.

Ausgeprägt individuelle Lösungen von überdurchschnittlicher architektonischer Qualität finden sich am ehesten unter den Fachgeschäften. Dabei ist die Größe des Ladens weit weniger ausschlaggebend als das konsequente Bemühen um eine unverwechselbare eigene Note. Der Bildteil dieses Bandes enthält eine ganze Reihe von Beispielen, bei denen auf knappstem Raum eine großzügige, einprägsame Wirkung erzielt wurde. Das Fachgeschäft mit seinem spezialisierten Angebot lebt auch heute noch von dem Bestreben, jeden Kundenwunsch auf persönliche Weise zu befriedigen. Individuelle Bedienung, sachverständige Fachberatung und zusätzliche Service-Leistungen sollen den Verbraucher als Stammkunden an das Unternehmen binden. In diesem emotionalen Prozeß spielt die Ladengestaltung eine wichtige Rolle. Sie prägt die Atmosphäre und beeinflußt das Image eines Geschäftes. Sie kann gewisse Stimmungswerte aktivieren: Verspieltheit in der Modeboutique, saloppe Nonchalance im Teenager-Studio, solide Eleganz im Schuhhaus oder präzise Sachlichkeit im Photoladen. Die Architektur wird zum Stimmungsträger, der durch entsprechende Materialwahl, Beleuchtung, Farb- und Formgebung wesentlich dazu beiträgt, die Ware in Szene zu setzen. Das Gehäuse ist hier keineswegs die anonyme, nur zufällig wahrgenommene Begrenzung der Nutzfläche, sondern die mehr oder minder kunstvolle Fassung für das jeweilige Warenprogramm. Dabei sind der schöpferischen Phantasie des Innenarchitekten eigentlich nur dort Grenzen gesetzt, wo die architektonische Hülle zum Selbstzweck, zur Attraktion an sich wird. Das Schuhgeschäft I. Miller in New York (Abb. 2) macht bei aller Originalität die Problematik einer solchen Überspitzung deutlich. Säulen, Brüstungen und Decke des im Mittelteil über 10 m hohen Raumes sind mit biegsamen, schuppenartig nebeneinander liegenden Holzleisten verkleidet, die an die Bündelpfeiler und Fächergewölbe mittelalterlicher Kirchen erinnern: eine Kathedrale des Einzelhandels, in der der Verkauf von Schuhen zelebriert wird.

Der firmeneigene Ausstellungsraum, die zweite Gruppe unserer Beispielsammlung, zeigt noch ausgeprägter als das Fachgeschäft die Tendenz, die Präsentation des Produkts mit der Repräsentation des Unternehmens zu verbinden. Als Bauaufgabe läßt der Showroom dem Architekten den größeren Spielraum. Das Bestreben, durch Originalität der Gestaltung Fortschrittlichkeit und Aufgeschlossenheit zu dokumentieren, verhilft manchem avantgardistischen Projekt zur Verwirklichung. Dazu kommt, daß der Entwerfer eines Showrooms meist mit einem großzügig bemessenen Budget

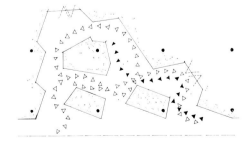

9. Ideal plan for the layout of an entrance bay with slanted glasswalls, asymmetrically placed entrances and island-type show-cases (design by Eduard Schrag. From 'Baumeister', August 1962).

9. Idealschema für die Anlage einer Schaufensterbucht mit abgeschrägten Glaswänden, asymmetrisch liegenden Eingängen und inselförmigen Vitrinen. (Entwurf Eduard Schrag. Nach: »Baumeister«, August 1962).

10. In the exclusive fashion shop closed cupboards contain the goods. Shop assistants offer the customer a selection. The value of the goods is raised psychologically, their speciality underlined (see p. 16).

10. Im exklusiven Modegeschäft nehmen geschlossene Schränke die Ware auf. Bedienungspersonal legt eine Auswahl vor. Psychologische Aufwertung der Waren, deren Besonderheit betont wird (siehe Seite 16).

11. Fashion shop in the style of Carnaby Street, London. Casual, open display in an apparently improvised, unconventional setting (shop belonging to Marion Foale and Sally Tuffin, London).

11. Mode-Shop im Stil der Londoner Carnaby Street. Saloppes, offenes Angebot in improvisiert wirkendem, unkonventionellem Ladenmilieu (Laden von Marion Foale und Sally Tuffin, London).

rechnen kann. Von der betriebstechnischen Seite her wird seine Planung dadurch erleichtert, daß kein komplettes Warensortiment mit dem erforderlichen Stapel- und Lagerraum unterzubringen ist, sondern nur eine vergleichsweise kleine Anzahl von Schau- und Demonstrationsobjekten. Große Unternehmen, die einem breiten Publikum bekannt sind, können es sich sogar erlauben, die Ausstellungsobjekte ganz beiläufig zu behandeln und das Schwergewicht auf die Raumkomposition zu legen. Die Olivetti-Filiale in Venedig (Abb. 3 und 4) bietet dafür ein Beispiel. Im nahezu leeren Erdgeschoß, das sein Gepräge durch edle Materialien – Marmorwände und Glasmosaikboden – bekommt, dominieren zwei Akzente, die sich nur assoziativ mit der Produktion in Verbindung bringen lassen: eine Metallplastik mit spiegelnden Wölbungen und eine aus polierten Betonblöcken gefügte Treppe, die als kristalline Struktur eine Art Kontrapunkt bildet. Im Bewußtsein der gesicherten Marktposition verzichtet eine solche Lösung fast ganz darauf, dem Passanten konkrete Produktinformationen zu geben; sie suggeriert in erster Linie Prestigewerte: Eleganz, Präzision, Exklusivität. Im Ausland dosieren die Olivetti-Vertretungen das Mischungsverhältnis von Information und Repräsentation stärker zugunsten des Produkts, wovon die Ausstellungsräume in Barcelona (Seite 66) oder Paris (Seite 63) einen Eindruck vermitteln. Zusammen mit dem noch immer zu den Spitzenleistungen des Ausstellungsdesign gehörenden New Yorker Showroom (Abb. 5) demonstrieren die Olivetti-Niederlassungen die Möglichkeit, jede Filiale in einer anderen Handschrift zu gestalten, wozu die bedeutendsten italienischen Architekten herangezogen werden. Den entgegengesetzten Weg geht beispielsweise die Porzellanfabrik Rosenthal. Die Ausstattung ihrer »Studiohäuser« (Abb. 6 und Seite 100) ist wie ein Markenartikel behandelt. Die Ausstellungsräume in Paris, Zürich oder Berlin unterscheiden sich nur in Nuancen, hinter denen immer die Konstante des einheitlichen Firmengesichts sichtbar bleibt.

Während der Showroom die repräsentative Komponente des Fachgeschäftes verstärkt, steht bei der dritten Gruppe von Beispielen, die für diesen Band ausgewählt wurden, mehr der Service im Vordergrund. Ob Friseur- oder Schönheitssalon, Reisebüro oder Ticket Office einer Fluggesellschaft, es sind Dienstleistungsbetriebe, die ihren Kunden Beratung und Betreuung verkaufen. Die Räume, in denen der Besucher empfangen wird, sollen sein Interesse wecken, seine Erwartung steigern, ihn einstimmen auf das, was man ihm zu bieten hat. Das »Wie« des Angebots wird genauso wichtig wie die Leistung an sich. Sitzen die Akzente richtig, so kann dieses »Wie« im Unterbewußtsein des Kunden eine ganze Skala positiver Reaktionen auslösen: die Selbstbestätigung gesellschaftlicher Exklusivität, das Hochgefühl, mit dazu zu gehören, die Befriedigung, sich etwas leisten zu können, oder auch nur das einfache Wohlbehagen darüber, in einer erfreulichen Umgebung fachkundig umsorgt zu werden – jedenfalls alles Empfindungen, die der Bereitschaft, Geld auszugeben, förderlich sind. Wie unsere Beispiele deutlich machen – etwa die auf den Seiten 142 und 148 wiedergegebenen Friseursalons –, führen die unterschiedlichsten Wege zu diesem Ziel. Das sachlich-intellektuelle Klima eines Damensalons im Londoner Business District, der auf Sekretärinnen und Mannequins spezialisiert ist, spricht seine Kundinnen ebenso treffsicher an wie der italienische Coiffeursalon, bei dem einzelne Rundnischen das Gefühl geben, besonders bevorzugt bedient zu werden; sie sind aber doch so gruppiert, daß der Kontakt zu den Nachbarkabinen möglich ist. Beide Beispiele sind typisch für das Bemühen, dem Kunden ein eigenständiges, unverwechselbares Ambiente zu bieten, dessen Atmosphäre sich deutlich von der landläufigen Dutzendlösung unterscheidet.

Am leichtesten haben es hierbei die Agenturen von Touristenorganisationen und Luftfahrtlinien, die für ein bestimmtes Land oder eine bestimmte nationale Fluggesellschaft werben. Sie können auf die Anziehungskraft einer folkloristisch gefärbten Ladengestaltung bauen, wobei natürlich das Farbplakat und die quadratmetergroße Photographie allein ebensowenig genügen wie irgendein zufällig vorhandenes Museumsstück auf der Empfangstheke. Auch eine Häufung derartiger Accessoires ergibt noch lange keine überzeugende moderne Lösung. Diese würde voraussetzen, daß es gelingt, die verschiedenen Elemente in den Gesamtentwurf zu integrieren. Einen solchen »Total Design« zeigt beispielsweise die Frankfurter Niederlassung der Israel Airlines (Abb. 7 und Seite 161). Hebräische und lateinische Buchstaben variieren vom Leuchtwürfel vor der Fassade bis zur Reliefwand in den verschiedensten Kombinationen den Namen der Fluggesellschaft EL-AL. Die sparsame, durch den Pflasterboden und die Rauhputzwände rustikal wirkende Oberflächenbehandlung weckt zusammen mit den Kakteen und dem zur Wandskulptur vergrößerten Brustschild eines jüdischen Hohepriesters unaufdringliche Assoziationen an Landschaft und Kultur Israels. Die Decke aus stilisierten Flugzeugen weist, ohne die formale Einheit zu sprengen, auf den speziellen Zweck des Raumes hin.

Wo es nicht nur um reale Bedarfsdeckung geht wie beim Besuch eines Lebensmittel-Supermarktes, und wo nicht ein vorgefaßter Kaufwunsch befriedigt werden soll, da steht am Anfang allen Verkaufens die Notwendigkeit, die indifferente Haltung eines Passanten in wachsendes Interesse zu verwandeln und ihn schließlich so weit zu bringen, daß er als potentieller Kunde den Laden betritt. An diesem Verwandlungsprozeß ist in erster Linie das Auge beteiligt. Die Ladengestaltung beginnt also damit, das Warenangebot möglichst attraktiv und umfassend vor das Auge des Passanten zu bringen – eine Funktion, die das Schaufenster, die Ausstellungsvitrine oder auch die ganze Frontseite des Ladens übernimmt, wenn sie in voller Breite und ausreichender Höhe ausschließlich aus Glas besteht und damit den ganzen Innenraum zu einem einzigen Schaufenster macht. Mit diesem Öffnen nach außen bestreiten beispielsweise deutsche und schweizerische Ladengestalter so ausgiebig ihr Repertoire, daß manche Fachleute die weitgehende Übereinstimmung schon wieder als monoton empfinden. Eloxiertes Aluminium wird ebenso reichlich verwendet wie Glas-Schaufenster bis auf den Gehweg herunter, Nur-Glas-Türen, Glaslaibungen, Ganzglasvitrinen: ein Ende dieses Trends läßt sich nicht absehen. Allenfalls können sich berühmte Spezialgeschäfte bei ihren Auslagen ein Understatement leisten. Der Verzicht auf eine unmittelbare Warenwerbung setzt jedoch einen außergewöhnlich hohen Bekanntheitsgrad von Angebot und Qualitätsstandard eines Unternehmens voraus. Der Architekt eines inzwischen weithin bekannt gewordenen Kerzenladens in Wien (Abb. 8 und Seite 94) ging in diese Richtung, als er die üblichen Auslagefenster auf zwei diagonal gestellte, nur noch leuchtschirmgroße Vitrinen zusammenschrumpfen ließ. Dafür gab er der aluminiumverkleideten Ladenfront eine so ausgeprägt expressive Form, daß diese in der Intensität des visuellen Appells jede »normale« Lösung übertrifft.

Im allgemeinen hält man sich jedoch an die bewährte Regel, mit möglichst viel Schaufensterfläche eine möglichst breite Übersicht über das aktuelle Warenangebot zu geben. Wo die knappe Frontlänge eines Gebäudes zu enge Grenzen setzt, wird zusätzliche Fensterfläche häufig durch Ausbuchten des Eingangsbereiches gewonnen. Schmalbrüstige Hausfronten lassen gar keine andere Wahl, selbst wenn kostbare Ladenfläche geopfert werden muß. Die Schaufensterbucht hat überdies den Vorteil, den Betrachter aus dem Passantenstrom herauszulösen. Er kann sein Tempo nach Belieben verlangsamen, ohne andere Fußgänger zu behindern. Das erbringt längere Stoppzeiten vor den Fenstern und damit größere Chancen für das Reifen eines Kaufwunsches. Die Psychologie hat herausgefunden, daß eine solche Bucht nicht tiefer als breit sein darf, wenn unterbewußtes Beengtsein cder gar Angstgefühle vermieden werden sollen. Sie plädiert auch für trichterförmig abge-

12, 13. Mirrors and mirror walls create the illusion of increased space (see pp 94 and 16).

12, 13. Spiegel und Spiegelwände schaffen illusionäre Raumerweiterungen (siehe Seite 94 und 16).

13

schrägte oder unregelmäßig gebrochene Wände, um nicht durch scharfe Winkel oder frontale »Sperren« eine Fluchtreaktion auszulösen, und sie schlägt vor, den Ladeneingang am tiefsten Punkt der Bucht asymmetrisch anzuordnen, weil Symmetrie eine bewußte Entscheidung verlange und dadurch die im Unterbewußtsein aufkeimende Kaufneigung reduziert würde. Der Architekt Eduard Schrag hat aus diesen Überlegungen ein Idealschema abgeleitet (Abb. 9), bei dem inselförmige Vitrinen eine zusätzliche erwünschte Lenkung der Bewegungsrichtung erbringen.

Eine besonders interessante Lösung bietet in diesem Zusammenhang das mobile Schaufenstersystem, das für das Düsseldorfer Rosenthal-Studiohaus entwickelt wurde (Seite 100). Ein in die Decke eingelassenes Gitternetz aus Führungsschienen ermöglicht es, genormte Schaufenster- und Vitrinenscheiben sowie dazu passende Wandtafeln und Glastüren in kurzer Zeit beliebig zu versetzen und damit den Grundriß der Schaufensteranlage und der Eingangszone über Nacht völlig zu verändern. Die Schaufensterfront läßt sich dabei auf mehr als das Fünffache der Hausbreite vergrößern. Die einzige Einschränkung, der dieses äußerst flexible System unterliegt, ist die, daß der Quadratraster der Deckenschienen keine Schrägstellung von Scheiben- und Plattenelementen erlaubt. Bei dem verhältnismäßig kleinen Modul von 70 × 70 cm fällt das aber kaum ins Gewicht.

Auf der zweiten Stufe verlagert sich das Werben um den Kunden in das Innere des Ladens; neben die optische Information tritt dort das Verkaufsgespräch, der unmittelbare Kontakt zwischen Verkäufer und potentiellem Käufer und – als weiteres wichtiges Stimulans für den endgültigen Kaufentschluß – die direkte Begegnung mit der Ware.

Der Grad, in dem das Verkaufspersonal dabei als Vermittler tätig wird, hat auch beim Fachgeschäft beträchtliche Rückwirkungen auf die Einrichtung. Das äußerste Extrem bildet das luxuriöse Spezialgeschäft, dessen Warenangebot bis auf wenige repräsentative Stücke in Schränken und Schubfächern verborgen wird. Das setzt einen Kundenkreis voraus, der seine Wünsche präzis zu formulieren weiß und eine ziemlich genaue Vorstellung über das mögliche Angebot hat. Es bedingt ferner geschultes Personal, das mit psychologischem Einfühlungsvermögen rasch den Kaufwunsch zu sondieren vermag und geeignet erscheinende Ware vorlegt. Erfahrung und Fingerspitzengefühl des Verkäufers entscheiden über die richtige Vorauswahl, und hierin liegt die mögliche Schwäche dieses Anbietesystems. Sein unbestrittener Vorteil ist die psychologische Aufwertung der Ware. Das einzelne Warenstück kann nachdrücklich in Szene gesetzt werden und gewinnt dadurch an Exklusivität. Dem Kunden wird suggeriert, wie sehr die vorgelegte Auswahl auf seine individuellen Ansprüche zugeschnitten ist. Die Haute Couture verkauft beispielsweise vorwiegend auf diese Weise. Innenarchitektonisch bedingt sie geschlossene, feste Einbauten, die als Schränke und Schubkastenelemente, als Kommoden und Theken vom Material und von der Farbe her so beherrschende Akzente setzen (Abb. 10), daß die übrige Raumgestaltung ihnen zwangsläufig untergeordnet werden muß.

Das andere Extrem ist das Fachgeschäft, das sein Angebot möglichst uneingeschränkt vor dem Kunden ausbreitet. Die Mode-Shops im Stil der Londoner Carnaby Street liefern dafür ein Beispiel (Abb. 11). Improvisierte Gestelle oder ganz simple Stangen dienen als Kleiderständer; ein alter Stuhl oder sonst ein Gegenstand aus der Rumpelkammer, zum Pop-Art-Gegenstand verfremdet, wird als Warenträger benutzt. Wand- und Deckenanstriche in kräftigen, ja knalligen Farben und mehr oder weniger skurrile Staffage-Objekte bestreiten zusammen mit den offen dargebotenen Modeartikeln die Ladengestaltung. Es herrscht eine burschikos-unkonventionelle Jahrmarktsstimmung, die konsequenterweise auch in der Umweltgestaltung zum Ausdruck kommt.

Die Verfechter der »Normallösung« gehen solchen Extremen aus dem Weg. Ihr Credo gipfelt in der Forderung nach Flexibilität. Flexibilität, um kurzfristig saisongebundene Artikel herausstellen zu können – Flexibilität, um langfristig allen Eventualitäten einer Sortimentserweiterung oder -verlagerung gewachsen zu sein. Ihr Ideal ist die variable Möblierung, das wandelbare Baukastensystem, die neutrale Farbgebung, die Rasterdecke mit gleichmäßiger Leuchtdichte. Und ihr Ergebnis ist leider nur zu oft: Langeweile und Sterilität. Die Auswahl für dieses Buch bemühte sich daher um Beispiele, bei denen Flexibilität nicht um den Preis ermüdender Gleichförmigkeit erkauft wurde. Vor allem aber konzentrierte sie sich auf Lösungen, die ernst machten mit dem Bestreben, ein unverwechselbares, individuelles Firmenprofil zu prägen. Es mag zutreffen, daß das oft nur auf Kosten der Wandlungsfähigkeit möglich war. Führende Marktforscher und Werbefachleute vertreten heute aber ohnehin die Ansicht, die Ladeneinrichtung müsse in wesentlich kürzeren Abständen erneuert werden, wenn man mit der Entwicklung im Einzelhandel Schritt halten wolle. Statt einen Entwurf durch allzu große Rücksichtnahme auf künftige Veränderungen zu verwässern (und zu verteuern), sei es ratsamer, von den eindeutig überschaubaren Gegebenheiten der Gegenwart auszugehen und einen rascheren Wechsel des Innenausbaus einzukalkulieren.

Aber auch heute schon haben Umbauten einen bedeutenden Anteil am Ladenbau. Besonders hoch ist der Prozentsatz an Modernisierungen bei den Fachgeschäften, die ihre angestammte Vorzugslage in der City nicht aufgeben wollen. Man sollte meinen, die vorgegebene Größe und Form der alten Ladenlokale sei kein geringes Handicap für die Neugestaltung. Wie jedoch der Bildteil dieses Bandes beweist, haben sich die Planer gerade durch solche Zwangssituationen zu den phantasievollsten Entwürfen anregen lassen. Fast in allen Fällen waren dabei zwei Hauptschwierigkeiten zu bewältigen: die Raumnot infolge ungenügender Nutzfläche und die Komplikationen, die sich aus ungünstigen Proportionen, toten Winkeln oder im Wege stehenden Konstruktionsgliedern ergaben. Neben den gebräuchlicheren Mitteln der Raumgliederung – etwa durch abgehängte Zwischendecken, Material-

14, 15. Unity of atmosphere by means of lighting installations: globe lamps in the laundry shop, studio projectors in the camera shop (see pp 22 and 86).

14, 15. Atmosphärische Einstimmung durch Lampenformen: Kugellampen im Wäschegeschäft, Atelierscheinwerfer im Photoladen (siehe Seite 22 und 86).

16, 17. Lighting installations and ceiling design as eye-catchers: lamps covered in spikes of aluminium plate, and internally-lit translucent cubes which form part of the ceiling system (see pp 24 and 68).

16, 17. Beleuchtungskörper und Deckenform als Blickfang: dornenförmige Lampenverkleidungen aus Aluminiumblech und von innen beleuchtete Schächte im kubischen Deckensystem (siehe Seite 24 und 68).

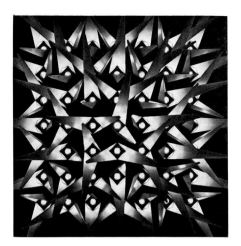 

und Farbwechsel an den Wänden oder durch Höhen- und Beleuchtungskontraste in den als Orientierungshilfe geschaffenen Zonen – wurden einfallsreiche Tricks angewandt, um durch scheinbares Aufheben oder Verschleiern der Raumgrenzen einen Laden größer wirken zu lassen. Sie reichen vom Trompe d'oeil perspektivischer Verkürzung (Seite 33) bis zum Vexierspiel mit gekurvten oder hexagonalen Binnenformen (Seite 142 und 60), die den ursprünglichen Rechteckraum absichtlich verunklären. Einige Beispiele, bei denen die optische Täuschung mit Spiegelwänden erzielt ist, verdienen besonders hervorgehoben zu werden. Da ist einmal der Wiener Kerzenladen (Abb. 12 und Seite 94), bei dem die Spiegelung in den schmalen Seitenfeldern nur eben aufblitzt, um für Sekundenbruchteile eine illusionäre Querachse zu bilden, wenn der Kunde in Längsrichtung durch den Laden geht. Und da ist die Modeboutique in Genua (Abb. 13 und Seite 16), bei der Spiegel und Gewölbe so raffiniert aufeinander bezogen sind, daß sich Illusion und Wirklichkeit nur mit Mühe unterscheiden lassen.
Solche Effekte lassen sich durch geschickte Beleuchtung wesentlich steigern. Es gibt eine weitverbreitete These, wonach die Beleuchtung dann am besten sei, wenn sie am wenigsten auffalle. Sieht man die Beispiele dieses Bandes daraufhin an, so ist man versucht, genau das Gegenteil zu postulieren. Überall dort, wo Einfallsreichtum und spezifische Atmosphäre dominieren, setzen die Formen der Beleuchtungskörper verstärkende Akzente: Kugellampen auf Wandarmen bringen einen Schuß »Belle Epoque« in das Wäschegeschäft (Abb. 14); schwere Atelierscheinwerfer an der Decke eines Photoladens erinnern an ein Filmstudio (Abb. 15); Deckenfelder mit beleuchteten Prismen (Abb. 16) und Kuben (Abb. 17) bilden nicht zu übersehende Blickfänge. Sie machen selbstverständlich die gleichmäßige Allgemeinbeleuchtung mit flächigen Leuchtfeldern, Kassettendecken oder aufgereihten Punktstrahlern nicht überflüssig, auch nicht die beweglichen Spotlights, mit denen das einzelne Warenstück ins rechte Licht gerückt wird. Doch stellen die Regeln für die richtige Leuchtdichte und Lichtfarbe des Normalfalls heute kaum mehr gestalterische Probleme. Die Industrie ist da mit einer Vielzahl von bewährten Lösungen zur Hand, die dem Publikum fahle Blässe und unnatürliche Gesichtsfarbe ersparen.

Für die Gruppierung der Beispiele wurde das einfachste, doch ergiebigste Prinzip gewählt: die Ordnung nach Branchen. In manchen Fällen rückt dadurch formal Ähnliches weit auseinander, auch lassen sich nationale Gemeinsamkeiten nicht so leicht aufspüren, wie es etwa bei einer Gliederung nach Ländern der Fall gewesen wäre. Dafür bietet die jetzige Reihenfolge unmittelbare Vergleichsmöglichkeiten unter verwandten Aufgabenstellungen. Nimmt man zum Beispiel die Gruppe der Photogeschäfte, so wird bei allen Unterschieden in der Größe, Form und Lage der Ladenräume deutlich, wie entschieden sich die Planer bemühten, jede basarähnliche Überfüllung zu vermeiden, und wie versucht wird, die kleinformatigen Apparate in größeren Blickfang-Einheiten (Kuppelvitrinen, Glastheken) zusammenzufassen. Oder die Möbelhäuser: Ihre Innenarchitekten waren alle bestrebt, mit einfachen, möglichst wandelbaren Elementen Raumandeutungen zu schaffen, die als neutraler Hintergrund die einzelnen Möbelstücke gegenseitig isolieren, ohne das Raumkontinuum der ganzen Ausstellungsfläche zu zerstören.
Allerdings sollte die Ordnung nach Branchen nicht zu eng verstanden werden. Ein Spezialgeschäft für Nähmaschinen gehört durchaus in die Nachbarschaft eines Showrooms, der elektrische Schreibmaschinen oder Lesegeräte für Mikrofilme zeigt. (In allen drei Fällen muß das Produkt einzeln herausgestellt werden, zugleich ist aber auch seine praktische Handhabung zu demonstrieren; das führt fast zwangsläufig zu einer Aufteilung in Ausstellungs- und Vorführbereich.) Eine Musikalienhandlung, in der Tausende von Noten, Taschenpartituren und Textbüchern bereitgehalten werden, stellt ähnliche Funktionsprobleme wie ein Reisebüro, wo eine Vielzahl von Prospekten und Katalogen griffbereit sein soll.
Solchen Wechselbeziehungen nachzugehen, über die engeren Branchenkategorien hinweg Analogien aufzudecken und sie vielleicht für das eigene Projekt nutzbar zu machen, dürfte für den planenden Architekten ebenso lohnend sein wie für den aufgeschlossenen Unternehmer.

15

Boutique in Genoa

Architect: Gianfranco Frattini, Milan

When this Abolaffio shop in an old palazzo in the heart of the city was redesigned, the architect gave it an atmosphere of considerable richness and fantasy by his ingenious use of mirrors – with the resulting interaction of spatial and optical planes – and by the leitmotif-like repetition of the vaulted ceilings. The sales area was more than doubled by the inclusion of the first floor and by the elimination of a space-consuming winding staircase. Both levels are connected by two straight flights of stairs running parallel with the wall and linked by a mezzanine which serves as a landing. The addition of this mezzanine contributes to the lively interplay of the vaulted wood-panelled ceilings.

Boutique für Damenmoden in Genua

Architekt: Gianfranco Frattini, Mailand

Beim Umbau dieses Ladenlokals der Firma Abolaffio, deren Geschäftsräume in einem alten Palazzo im Stadtzentrum von Genua untergebracht sind, gelang es dem Architekten, durch die raffinierte Anwendung von Spiegeltricks, durch räumliche oder optische Durchdringung und durch die leitmotivartige Wiederholung von Tonnengewölben ein außergewöhnlich reiches, geradezu phantastisch wirkendes Ambiente zu schaffen. Durch Einbeziehen des ersten Obergeschosses und Entfernen einer platzraubenden Wendeltreppe konnte die Verkaufsfläche mehr als verdoppelt werden. Beide Ebenen sind durch zwei parallel laufende, an der Wand liegende gerade Treppenzüge verbunden, die über ein Mezzaningeschoß führen, das als Treppenabsatz dient. Der Einbau dieses Zwischengeschosses bot die Möglichkeit zu dem reizvollen Spiel mit den gegeneinander versetzten, holzverschalten Tonnengewölben.

1. View from the mezzanine onto the ground floor. The mirrors above and below the elliptical opening reflect the upper vault – that of the mezzanine.

2–4. Plan of the first floor (top), mezzanine (centre), and ground floor. Storage cupboards with sliding doors have been built into the bases of the vaulted ceilings.

5. The bricked-up arch above the side display window shows the height of the original ceiling.

6. The front of the shop with the entrance in the centre.

1. In den Spiegeln über und unter dem elliptischen Ausschnitt spiegelt sich das höher liegende Gewölbe des Mezzanins.

2–4. Grundriß von erstem Obergeschoß (oben), Mezzaningeschoß (Mitte) und Erdgeschoß. In den seitlichen Nischen unter den Gewölbeansätzen sind mit Schiebetüren verschlossene Schränke eingebaut.

5. Der gemauerte Bogen über dem Schaufenster an der Seitenfront läßt die Höhe der ursprünglichen Wölbung erkennen.

6. Hauptfront mit Eingang (Mitte).

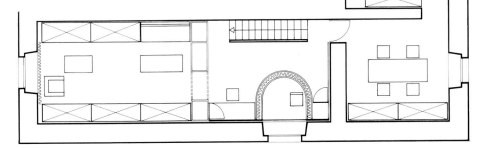

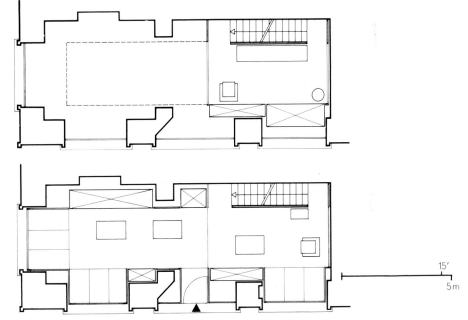

15'
5m

7. View of the ground-floor sales room. The mirror in the background of the photograph reflects the side display window, giving an impression that the room is of almost unlimited length. The walls contain storage cupboards. Foreground right, next to the sliding-door of one of the storage cupboards, is the shop entrance; almost opposite, behind the panelled wall, are the stairs. The first opening leads to the workshop in the cellar, the second to the mezzanine. The panelling on both the ceilings and the walls is of rosewood; the doors of the storage cupboards and part of the walls are covered in beige linen, and the floors have fitted carpets.

8. View of the elliptical 'eye' of the mezzanine, the balustrade of which is faced on both sides with mirrors (cf. pl. 7). The difference in height of the vaults over the ground floor and the mezzanine is shown.

7. Blick in den Erdgeschoß-Verkaufsraum. Optische Raumerweiterung durch Spiegelwand im Hintergrund, in der sich das Schaufenster an der Schmalseite reflektiert; dadurch scheinbare Aufhebung der Raumbegrenzung in der Längsachse. In den Längswänden Einbauschränke für die Ware. Vorn rechts im Anschluß an die Schrank-Schiebetür der Ladeneingang. Schräg gegenüber hinter der horizontal verschalten Wandscheibe die Treppe (vordere Türöffnung: Abgang zur Werkstatt im Keller; hintere Öffnung: Treppenaufgang zum Mezzaningeschoß). Holzleisten der Wand- und Deckenverschalung aus Jacaranda-Palisander, Schranktüren und Teile der Wände mit beigem Leinen bespannt. Teppichboden.

8. Blick auf das elliptische Mezzanin-»Auge«, dessen Brüstung beiderseits (siehe Abb. 7) mit Spiegeln verkleidet ist. Der Höhenunterschied zwischen den beiden Holztonnen über Erdgeschoß und Mezzanin ist deutlich zu erkennen.

9. Three-dimensional section through the ground floor, mezzanine, and first floor.
10. Due to the mirrors, the atmosphere of fantasy common to all the rooms reaches labyrinthine, surrealist proportions on the mezzanine. A bunch of flowers partly conceals the 'eye'.
11–13. Three details from the sales room on the first floor which is divided into halves by a glass-sided show-case. The lower and narrower connecting door echoes the ceiling motif, which appears again in the curtained fitting-room with its double semicircular wooden tracks, between which the drapery is guided.

9. Perspektivischer Schnitt durch Erdgeschoß, Mezzaningeschoß und Obergeschoß.
10. Die phantastische Atmosphäre, die alle Räume auszeichnet, verdichtet sich im Mezzaningeschoß durch die Reflektion der Spiegelwände zu einer labyrinthischen, surrealen Impression. Ein Blumenstrauß verdeckt das »Auge« teilweise.
11–13. Drei Detailansichten aus dem Verkaufsraum im ersten Obergeschoß, der durch eine doppelseitig verglaste Ausstellungsvitrine in zwei Hälften geteilt ist. Die niedrige und schmälere Verbindungstür variiert auch hier das Thema der Wölbungs- und Bogenformen in verschiedenen Höhen. Eine mit Vorhängen verschließbare Kabine für Anproben wandelt das Bogenmotiv durch eine halbkreisförmige Führungsschiene aus Holz ab, zwischen deren Doppelholmen die Vorhänge angebracht sind.

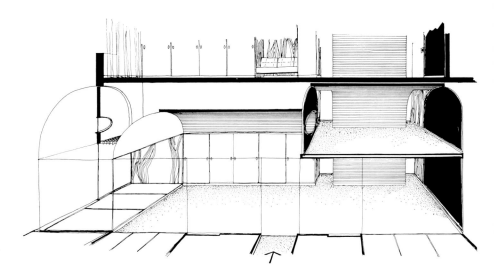

Dress Shop in Nottingham

Architects: Diamond, Redfern and Partners, London, Wolverhampton, Nottingham

The problem was to rebuild, within a limited budget, two separate spaces that were in a dilapidated state and connected only by a narrow corridor. The atmosphere of the new shop was to be sophisticated but not too exclusive. The space facing the street was designed as a display and reception area serving the preliminaries of sale. The second space houses storage racks, fitting cubicles and staff rooms. Rather than obstruct the view into the interior with the back wall of a display window, the dresses on display are simply mounted on a low square platform covered with grey fitted carpet matching the rest of the floor. The wall panelling of natural softwood unifies the various planes, providing a feeling of continuity, and a neutral but lively foil to the articles on display.

Fachgeschäft für Damenkonfektion in Nottingham

Architekten: Diamond, Redfern and Partners, London, Wolverhampton, Nottingham

Zwei lediglich durch einen schmalen Durchgang miteinander verbundene Räume in ziemlich schlechtem baulichem Zustand waren ohne großen Kostenaufwand umzubauen. Dabei sollte eine zwar anspruchsvolle, aber nicht zu exklusive Atmosphäre geschaffen werden. Der zur Straße gelegene Raum wurde für Ausstellungszwecke und einführende Verkaufsgespräche vorgesehen, der zweite Raum umfaßt die notwendigen Kleiderregale, Umkleidekabinen und ein Personalabteil. Um den Blick in den Laden nicht durch Schaufensterrückwände zu verstellen, ist die sehr sparsam dekorierte Ausstellung auf ein niedriges, quadratisches Podium verlegt, das wie der übrige Raum einen grauen Spannteppich trägt. Die Wandverkleidung aus naturfarbenen Tannenholzbrettern faßt die verschiedenen Winkelflächen kontinuierlich zusammen und gibt eine neutrale, aber doch lebendige Folie für die ausgestellten Kleidungsstücke.

1. View from the street. Blockboard lettering painted white is bolted to the plate glass window. A matt black band, two boards deep, running round the perimeter of the room, emphasizes the display recesses and draws one's eye towards the fitting-room in the rear. The spotlights for the display platform are mounted on two black wooden cross-beams. General lighting by fluorescent tubes is concealed behind wooden fascias. For woollens – a movable display counter with mahogany and panels. Khaki curtains, mustard-coloured ceiling, grey fitted carpet.

1. Ansicht von der Straße. Weiß bemalte Holzbuchstaben mit Bolzen in Bohrlöchern der Schaufensterscheibe befestigt. Ein zwei Brettbreiten hohes, mattschwarzes Band betont die Oberkante der Warenetalagen und weist als Blickleitlinie zu dem Anproberaum im Hintergrund. An zwei quer durch den Raum gespannten schwarzen Balken sind die Spots für das Ausstellungspodium montiert. Übrige Raumbeleuchtung indirekt durch Leuchtstoffröhren hinter Holzblenden. Theke für Wollsachen schwenkbar, Seitenteile Mahagoni. Vorhang khakifarben, Decke senffarben, Spannteppich grau.

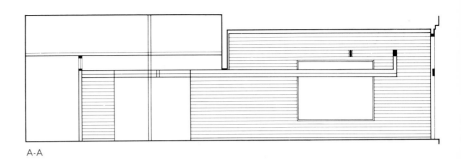

A-A

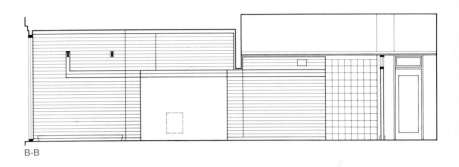

B-B

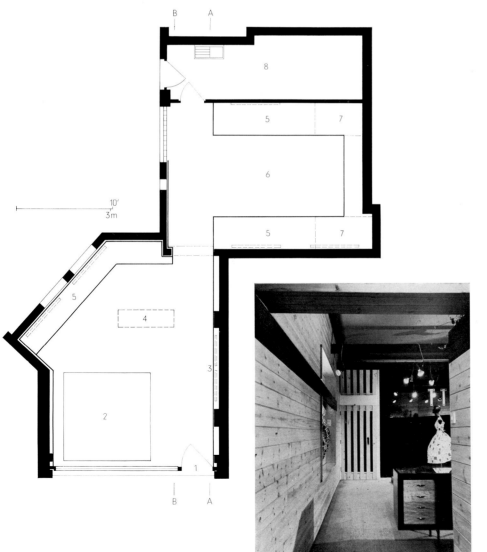

2. Interior elevation A–A of wall to right of entrance.
3. Interior elevation B–B of wall to left of entrance.
4. Floor plan. Key: 1 Entrance, 2 Display platform, 3 Display recess, 4 Movable counter for woollens, 5 Drawer space, 6 Fitting-room, 7 Changing cubicles, 8 Staff accommodation.
5, 6. Entrance door made of pine slats alternating with glass strips, with a ventilation hopper above.

2. Längsschnitt A–A und Ansicht der Eingangsseite.
3. Längsschnitt B–B und Ansicht der Podiumsseite.
4. Grundriß. Legende: 1 Eingang, 2 Ausstellungspodium, 3 Ausstellungsnische, 4 schwenkbare Theke für Wollsachen, 5 Schrankraum für Ware, 6 Anprobe, 7 Umkleidekabinen, 8 Personalraum.
5, 6. Eingangstür aus Tannenbrettern und Glasstreifen im Wechsel, darüber Klappflügel.

Shop for Underwear and Knitted Goods in Milan

Architects: Gian Antonio and Emiliano Bernasconi, Milan

The sales room of Biraghi & Co. in the Via Ugo Foscolo occupy the ground floor and the gallery of a corner building. Since the gallery extends over only part of the ground floor, the outer edge is two storeys high. The strong form of the free-standing cantilevered staircase constructed round the lift well, links the two planes. The sequence of plastic forms and uncluttered space characterizes the rest of the interior design. For functional reasons the goods themselves are stacked on shelves in card-board boxes which are arranged to form plain panels of colour. Luminous panels distributed at random over the ceiling, as well as mirrors, dark wood trim and spherical lamps enliven the rather formal atmosphere.

Fachgeschäft für Wäsche und Strickwaren in Mailand

Architekten: Gian Antonio und Emiliano Bernasconi, Mailand

Die Verkaufsräume der Firma Biraghi & Co. in der Via Ugo Foscolo nehmen das Erdgeschoß und die Empore eines Ecklokals ein, wobei die Galerie nur einen Teil der Grundfläche überspannt. Auf diese Weise reicht die Randzone des Erdgeschosses großenteils durch zwei Stockwerke. Eine frei im Raum stehende, um den Fahrstuhlschacht herumgeführte, auskragende Treppenkonstruktion stellt die Verbindung zwischen den beiden Ebenen her; zugleich wurde sie als expressive plastische Form in den Gesamtentwurf eingegliedert. Der Wechsel von plastischem Volumen und Leere bestimmt auch die übrige Einrichtung, obwohl die Ware selbst, in Kartons gleicher Größe auf Regalen gestapelt, aus funktionalen Gründen zu rein flächigen Partien zusammengefaßt ist. Unregelmäßig verteilte Decken-Leuchtwannen, Spiegel, dunkle Holzprofile und Kugellampen lockern auf, ohne die noble Atmosphäre zu beeinträchtigen.

1. The outer part of the ground floor rising two storeys high. Shelves and counters of dark wood; wood panels faced with red parchment-like plastic sheet screen the brick walls. At the left exterior wall, louvre blinds divide the display windows to form internal showcases.
2. View from the gallery.
3. Sales area under the gallery. A mirror elongates the luminous ceiling.
4. Staircase and lift well.
5. Street view. At right, the stair well.

1. Die zweigeschossige Randzone. Regale und Theken aus dunklem Holz, vor Mauerteilen Holzpaneele mit Verkleidung aus rot getönter, pergamentähnlicher Kunststoff-Folie, an linker Außenwand Ausstellungsvitrinen, die durch Halbieren der Schaufenster mittels Lamellenjalousien entstehen.
2. Blick von der Empore.
3. Verkaufsbereich unter der Empore. Ein Spiegel verlängert die Leuchtdecke.
4. Treppe und Aufzugturm.
5. Straßenansicht. Rechts der Treppenturm.

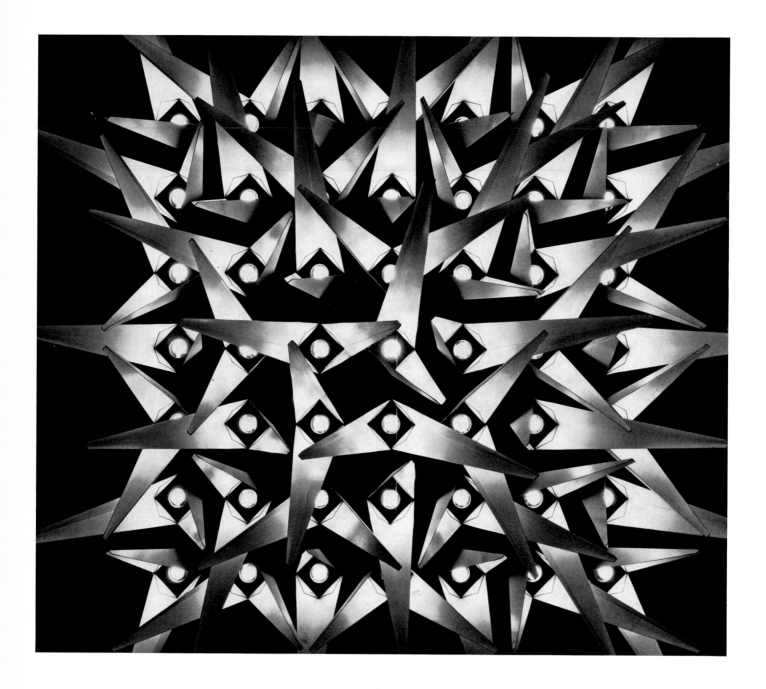

Men's Shop in Knightsbridge, London

Architects: B. & N. Westwood, Piet & Partners, London

The Austin Reed men's shop occupies most of the ground and first floor of an office building in the Brompton Road. The front consists of deep display windows, enclosed on three sides, alternating with slightly smaller and narrower windows, left open at the back which allow one to see right into the interior of the shop. Two mullions divide the latter type of window into three sections and provide supports for the adjustable display shelves. On the ground floor, where chiefly suits, shirts, hosiery, pullovers, sportswear and gifts are sold, the architects wanted to create an atmosphere that encourages the customer to look around without making him feel obliged to buy something. The focal point of the shop is the central staircase leading to the first floor and the departments for ready-to-wear clothing, coats, tailor-made suits, shoes and hats.

Herrenausstattungsgeschäft in Knightsbridge, London

Architekten: B. & N. Westwood, Piet & Partners, London

Das Herrenausstattungsgeschäft der Austin Reed Ltd. nimmt den überwiegenden Teil des Erdgeschosses und des ersten Obergeschosses eines Bürogebäudes ein, das an der Brompton Road in bester Geschäftslage erbaut wurde. In der Schaufensterfront wechseln tiefere, auf drei Seiten geschlossene Fenster mit etwas schmaleren, flachen Feldern, die den freien Einblick in das Innere erlauben; sie sind durch zwei Vertikalsprossen unterteilt, zwischen denen verstellbare Fachborde eingesetzt werden können. Im Erdgeschoß, wo in der Hauptsache Hemden, Strümpfe, Pullover, Sport- und Geschenkartikel verkauft werden, wurde eine Atmosphäre angestrebt, die den Kunden ohne Kaufzwang zum Umschauen einlädt. Blickpunkt ist die zentral gelegene Haupttreppe zum Obergeschoß, wo die Abteilungen für Herrenkonfektion, Maßkleidung, Schuhe und Hüte untergebracht sind.

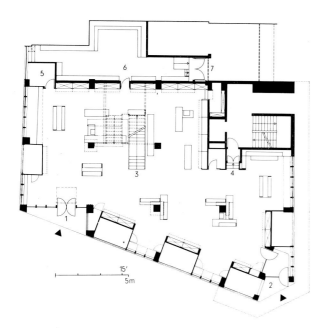

1. Looking up at the aluminium ceiling lights (designed by John McCarthy) above the stair-well. The reflective fins are of varying length.
2. Plan of ground floor. Key: 1 Main entrance, 2 Side entrance, 3 Main staircase, 4 Exit to lavatories, 5 Office, 6 Stockroom, 7 Service entrance.
3. View of the first floor and the staircase. Balustrade panels of smoked glass; visible woodwork chiefly in teak; floor areas liable to heavy wear in slate, the rest with fitted carpets. Electric underfloor heating.
4. Overall view of the shop which is flanked by side-streets. The first floor exterior consists of a high wall of precast concrete panels surmounted by a narrow strip window. Behind this wall are clothes racks. On the ground floor, to the left, the recessed main entrance; to the right, the side entrance with its canopy.

1. Untersicht der mit verschieden langen Dornenpaaren aus Aluminiumblech verkleideten Lampen über dem Treppenhaus. Entwurf: John McCarthy.
2. Grundriß des Erdgeschosses. Legende: 1 Haupteingang, 2 Nebeneingang, 3 Haupttreppe, 4 Ausgang Waschräume, 5 Büro, 6 Lager, 7 Lieferanteneingang.
3. Einblick in das Obergeschoß mit Treppenhaus, dessen Brüstungsfelder aus Rauchglasplatten bestehen. Holzteile überwiegend Teak, stark begangene Flächen mit Schieferplatten belegt, sonst Spannteppiche. Elektrische Fußbodenheizung.
4. Gesamtansicht des zwischen zwei Seitenstraßen liegenden Geschäfts. Obergeschoß bis auf ein schmales Fensterband mit verschieden breiten Betonplatten geschlossen; dahinter Kleiderständer. Im Erdgeschoß links der zurückgesetzte Haupteingang, rechts unter dem Vordach Nebeneingang.

5. View of the ground floor. The afrormosia counters have satin-finished stainless steel legs, and are freely distributed throughout the sales area. On the left, the main staircase.

6. The open and enclosed display windows as seen from inside the shop.

7. Rear of the staircase seen from the ground floor. The glass screen with its coloured plastic decoration provides a contrast with the teak panelling of the walls.

5. Längsblick durch das Erdgeschoß mit den inselförmig frei aufgestellten Verkaufstischen aus Afrormosia und seidenmatten Stahlgestellen. Links die Haupttreppe.

6. Die geschlossenen und offenen Schaufensterboxen vom Innenraum aus gesehen.

7. Außenseite des Treppenhauses im Erdgeschoß. Wandschirm aus Glasfeldern, mit farbigen Kunststoffplättchen dekoriert als Gegengewicht zur Teakholzverkleidung der übrigen Wände.

Store for Ladies' Wear in Richmond, Surrey

Architects: Conran Design Group, London
(Chief Designer: Rodney Fitch)

Fachgeschäft für Damenmoden in Richmond, Surrey

Architekten: Conran Design Group, London
(Entwurfsleitung: Rodney Fitch)

The Peter Robinson branch store in George Street was made from two older shops which, by re-planning and extensive structural alterations, were combined into one large sales area occupying two floors. The ground floor and the first floor are linked by a generously proportioned stairwell. Shopfitting costs were kept to a minimum by economical detailing and the use of inexpensive natural materials; for instance the niches with the hanging cases for dresses and coats were made of chipboard panels fixed to a soft-wood framing. The whole interior structure is based on a 2 ft 6 in module. Around the perimeter of the walls, there is a pine pelmet at 7 ft from the floor, behind which fluorescent tubes are mounted. The wall panels above the pelmet are removable.

Die Filiale der Firma Peter Robinson an der George Street entstand durch den Umbau zweier älterer Läden, die durch einschneidende bauliche Veränderungen in großzügige, zusammenhängende Verkaufsflächen verwandelt wurden. Sie erstrecken sich über zwei Stockwerke, wobei Erdgeschoß und Obergeschoß durch ein weiträumiges Treppenhaus verbunden sind. Die Kosten für die Inneneinrichtung konnten durch ökonomische Detailplanung und die Verwendung einfacher Materialien niedrig gehalten werden; so bestehen beispielsweise die Nischen für die aufgehängten Kleidungsstücke aus Preßspanplatten, die an einer einfachen Holzkonstruktion befestigt wurden. Alle Einbauten basieren auf einem Modul von rund 75 cm. Entlang der Außenwände ist in einer Höhe von 2,10 m eine Tannenholzblende angebracht, hinter der Leuchtröhren verdeckt montiert sind. Die aus farbigen Flächen und Fotos bestehenden Wandtafeln darüber sind abnehmbar.

1. View into a sales-room. Wood framed recesses for clothes racks along the walls; behind the wood pelmet fluorescent tubes illuminate the recesses which have exchangeable panels painted in different colours or decorated with photostats. General lighting by fluorescent tubes mounted between the rough sawn slats of the suspended wood ceiling. Spotlights and spherical lamps as additional light sources. The floor covered with a fitted dark grey sisal carpet.
2. The staircase with treads and balustrade of solid oak. The width of the 'mood' photostats corresponds to the basic module.
3. Detail of the recesses with wood framing and suspended slatted ceiling.

1. Blick in einen Verkaufsraum. An den Wänden entlang die Holzkonstruktion mit den Kleiderregalen; hinter den Holzblenden Leuchtröhren für die Nischen, darüber austauschbare Wandfelder mit farbigem Anstrich oder Großphotos. Deckenbeleuchtung aus Leuchtröhren zwischen den sägerauhen Latten der untergehängten Holzdecke. Punktstrahler und Kugellampen als Zusatzbeleuchtung. Fußboden mit dunkelgrauem Sisalteppich bespannt.
2. Das Treppenhaus mit Stufen und Brüstung aus massiven Eichenbrettern. Die Phototafeln mit Motiven zur Einstimmung entsprechen in der Breite dem Modul.
3. Ausschnitt mit der in Holz ausgeführten Nischenkonstruktion und der untergehängten Lattendecke.

1. Floor plan with entrance, sales areas and adjoining stockroom.
2. The entrance 'patio' with the show-cases.
3. View of the interior (see page 32).

1. Grundriß mit Eingangszone, Verkaufsbereichen
und anschließendem Lagerraum.
2. Der »Eingangspatio« mit den Vitrinen.
3. Blick in den Innenraum (siehe Seite 32).

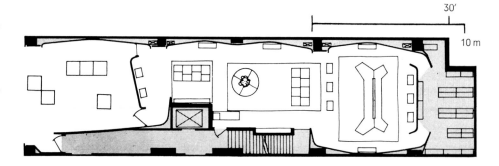

30'

10 m

Chilean Shoe Store in New York

Architects: Morris Ketchum Jr & Associates,
New York, N. Y.

The single-storey shop, in which the Santiago Shoe & Leather Corporation present their products to the US market, occupies the ground floor of a narrow, deep Fifth Avenue building. It serves concurrently as a salesroom for individual clients and as a wholesale showroom. The shop front is a large, open-fronted, funnel-shaped recess, the walls of which converge towards the main entrance. The usual display windows were dispensed with, and the shoes are exhibited in six square glass show-cases, which stand on circular columns and extend to the ceiling. For greatest effect they were arranged in echelon. The width of the entrance was enlarged still further by setting back the doorway leading to the upper floors. Separate carpets serve to divide the interior into two sales areas.

Chilenisches Schuhgeschäft in New York

Architekten: Morris Ketchum Jr. & Associates,
New York, N. Y.

Der eingeschossige Laden, in dem die Santiago Shoe & Leather Corporation ihre Produkte auf dem US-Markt vorstellt, nimmt das Erdgeschoß eines schmalen, tiefen Gebäudes an der Fifth Avenue ein. Er dient zugleich als Verkaufsraum für Einzelkunden und als Ausstellungsraum für Großhändler. Dem eigentlichen Laden ist eine große Nische vorgeschaltet, deren gekurvte Wände sich in der Tiefe trichterförmig verengen und in eine massive Querwand übergehen. Auf die üblichen Schaufenster ist verzichtet; statt dessen wird das Warenangebot in sechs auf Rundsäulen gestellten quadratischen Glasvitrinen präsentiert, die bis zur Decke reichen. Sie staffeln sich in der Tiefe der an einen Patio erinnernden Eingangsbucht, die in ihrem vorderen Bereich noch einmal zusätzlich verbreitert ist, da der Hauseingang zu den Obergeschossen hier zurückgesetzt wurde. Der Innenraum ist durch Teppiche in zwei Verkaufsbereiche unterteilt.

3. (Page 31) The serpentine side walls conceal the structural members and air-conditioning ducts. The breaks in them mark the division of the interior into two sales areas, for medium and high-priced shoes, without, however, destroying the continuity of the space. On the brown ceramic tile floor, rectangular carpets form three islands; on the two larger stand a circular seat set around a jardiniere, and a back-to-back double sofa. Cushioned benches and square display tables complete the furniture forming an intimate arrangement which, together with the entrance patio, creates a South American atmosphere. The entrance is screened by a partition wall made of rough-sawn wood strips stained dark brown, a treatment that is repeated in the narrower panels of the side walls.

4. View from the outer sales area looking towards the inner sales area. The dark wooden screen behind the sofa conceals the entrances of the passages to the stockrooms to right and left.

5. The wooden screen at the entrance to the shop. The greens and blues of the carpets and the cushions echo the colours of the shoe-boxes, which were also designed by the architects.

3. (Seite 31) Unterbrechungen in den gewellten Längswänden, hinter denen sich Stützen und Klimakanäle verbergen, deuten die Unterteilung des Innenraums in zwei Verkaufsbereiche für die mittlere und höhere Preisklasse an, ohne das Raumkontinuum zu beeinträchtigen. Rechteckige Teppiche sparen aus der mit braunen Keramikplatten belegten Bodenfläche drei Inseln aus, auf denen eine ringförmige Bank um einen Pflanzenbehälter und ein Rücken an Rücken gestelltes Doppelsofa stehen. Bänke mit Sitzkissen sowie quadratische Ausstellungstischchen vervollständigen das Mobiliar, das in seiner intim wirkenden Anordnung zusammen mit dem Eingangspatio südamerikanische Atmosphäre schafft. Der Eingang wird durch eine Trennwand aus rauh gesägten, tiefbraun gestrichenen Holzleisten abgeschirmt, ein Motiv, das sich an den Seitenwänden mit schmaleren Panels wiederholt.

4. Blick vom vorderen Verkaufsbereich auf die hintere Verkaufszone mit dem Doppelsofa vor der rückwärtigen, dunkel gebeizten Latten-Schirmwand, hinter der rechts und links Durchgänge zum Lagerraum führen.

5. Der Holzscreen am Eingang. Die Grün- und Blautöne der Teppiche und Kissenbezüge wiederholen die Farben der Schuhschachteln, die gleichfalls von den Architekten gestaltet wurden.

Shoe Shop in Florence

Architect: Pierluigi Spadolini, Florence

The Mantellassi shoe shop, which replaced an old store on the ground floor of a Florentine palazzo occupies an area only 13 ft wide and 36 ft deep. The main problem confronting the architect was that an arch-like opening about 6 ft wide had to accommodate both the entrance and the display window. He found an interesting solution by aligning part of the interior along the axis of the entrance to form a side aisle. The all-glass entrance door is flanked on both sides by showcases, lower in height than the door, which gradually decrease in depth as they recede from the facade. As one looks down this aisle (about 33 ft deep and 3 ft 4 in wide) one's gaze is finally stopped by the show-case in front of the white wall at the end of the showroom. Thus an entrance area was created which is very effective on account of its perspective and which, at the same time, serves as a display window. The materials used, and the architectural details, anticipate the interior of the shop.

Schuhgeschäft in Florenz

Architekt: Pierluigi Spadolini, Florenz

Der Einbau des Schuhgeschäftes Mantellassi in das nur etwa 4 m breite und 11 m tiefe Lokal im Erdgeschoß eines Florentiner Palazzos stellte insofern besondere Probleme, als für Eingang und Schaufenster lediglich eine Bogenöffnung von rund 2 m Breite zur Verfügung stand. Aus dieser Schwierigkeit fand der Architekt einen geschickten Ausweg, indem er einen Teil des Ladeninneren achsial auf den Eingang bezog. Durch die Ganzglastür, die beiderseits von niedrigeren, stufenweise schmäler werdenden Vitrinen flankiert wird, blickt man über einen 10 m tiefen, 1 m breiten Gang auf eine Vitrine mit weißer Rückwand. So entstand ein in der perspektivischen Verkürzung effektvoller Eingangsbereich, der zugleich die Aufgabe des Schaufensters übernimmt. In Material und Formensprache klingt hier schon die Lösung des Innenraumes an.

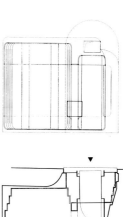

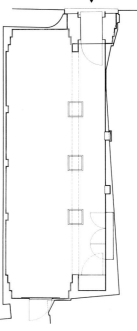

1. (Page 33) Three cubical glass show-cases mark the transition from the entrance aisle (visible from the street) to the actual sales area. The ceiling of the main room, which is higher than that of the side aisle, was dropped down over these cubical cases, to form a box-like beam which contains the ducts of the air-conditioning system and carries the square lighting fixtures. Floor-to-ceiling mirrors were placed at the two narrow ends of the sales room to make it appear still larger. The overall mood of the shop is set by the richly grained mahogany surfaces of walls, floor and ceiling. The panelling has been used to round off angles, and in the corners of the room itself, the normal right-angle has been replaced by a series of gradual steps (see pl. 2).
2. View towards the entrance side. On the left, in the background, the cashier's desk. Above the sales area, hexagonal light panels mounted flush with the ceiling.
3. Cross-section and floor plan.
4. The show-cases have bronzed brass frames and mahogany-veneered bases with the same rounded-off angles as the rest of the room.
5. The entrance through the arch seen from the street.

1. (Seite 33) Den Übergang zwischen der (von der Straße aus sichtbaren) Eingangszone zum eigentlichen Verkaufsraum markieren drei würfelförmige Glasvitrinen. Über ihnen wurde die über dem Seitengang und dem Hauptraum verschieden hohe Decke als balkenförmiger Kasten heruntergezogen, der die Kanäle der Klimaanlage und quadratische Leuchten aufnimmt. Die beiden Schmalseiten des Verkaufsraums tragen raumhohe Spiegel zur optischen Erweiterung. Der Raumeindruck wird bestimmt durch die Wand-, Boden- und Deckenverkleidung aus lebhaft gemasertem Mahagoniholz. An den Ecken wurde die Verschalung überall abgerundet. In den Winkeln zwischen Längs- und Schmalseiten ist sie außerdem stufenförmig abgetreppt.
2. Blick zur Eingangsseite. Links hinten die Kasse. Über dem Verkaufsraum sind Felder mit bündig liegenden, sechseckigen Leuchtkästen montiert.
3. Querschnitt und Grundriß.
4. Auch die Vitrinensockel bestehen aus Mahagoniholz, das ebenso wie die Ecken der Holzverkleidung gerundet wurde. Beschläge der Glaskästen aus bronziertem Messing.
5. Blick von der Straße auf den Eingang in der Bogenöffnung.

Shoe Store in Saarbrücken

Architects: Rolf Gutbier and Hans Kammerer,
Stuttgart
Assistant: Walter Belz

Schuhhaus in Saarbrücken

Architekten: Rolf Gutbier und Hans Kammerer,
Stuttgart
Mitarbeiter: Walter Belz

The newly-built Salamander branch store stands in the Bahnhofstrasse, the main shopping street of Saarbrücken. The area at the architects' disposal was only about 40 ft wide and 132 ft deep: of the depth, 50 ft had planning permission for six storeys, the remaining 82 ft for only two or three. The store and the stockroom are in the three bottom storeys which use the full depth of 132 feet; the rest is let as office space. As the building ajoining was constructed at the same time, the two share a common staircase up to the office level. This meant that the valuable frontage could be reserved for the store entrance and display windows. The illustrations show how the architects succeeded in giving the sales areas the greatest possible feeling of continuity and uncluttered space.

Für diesen Neubau einer Verkaufsfiliale der Salamander AG. an der Bahnhofstraße, der Hauptgeschäftsstraße Saarbrückens, stand ein Grundstück von nur 12 m Frontbreite bei 40 m Tiefe zur Verfügung. Es durfte lediglich auf einer Tiefe von 15 m sechsgeschossig gebaut werden, für die restlichen 25 m waren höchstens zwei bis drei Geschosse erlaubt. Laden und Lager sind in den drei auf die volle Tiefe von 40 m durchgehenden Geschossen untergebracht, der Rest wird als Bürofläche vermietet. Da das Nachbargrundstück gleichzeitig bebaut wurde, sind die Aufgänge zu den Bürogeschossen beider Gebäude in einem gemeinsamen Treppenhaus zusammengefaßt. So blieb die kostbare Straßenfront für Ladenzugang und Schaufenster erhalten. Die Abbildungen zeigen, wie die Absicht verwirklicht wurde, die Verkaufszonen möglichst großräumig und durchsichtig zu halten.

1. View, from the men s department, of the reception area and the passageway.
2. Longitudinal section: 1 Bahnhofstrasse, 2 Entrance recess, 3 Reception, 4 Childrens' department, 5 Men's department, 6 Women's department, 7 Stockroom, 8 Offices, 9 Apartment.
3–5. Plans of basement (bottom) ground floor and first floor: 1 Children's department, 2 Entrance recess, 3 Reception and packing table, 4 Cashdesk, 5 Men's department, 6 Immediate stock, 7 Manager's office, 8 Women's department, 9 Customers' lift, 10 Goods lift, 11 Back stairs, 12 Main staircase to offices.

1. Blick von der Herrenabteilung auf Empfangsbereich und Passage.
2. Längsschnitt: 1 Bahnhofstraße, 2 Passage, 3 Empfang, 4 Kinderabteilung, 5 Herrenabteilung, 6 Damenabteilung, 7 Lager, 8 Büros, 9 Wohnung.
3–5. Grundrisse von Untergeschoß (unten), Erdgeschoß und 1. Obergeschoß: 1 Kinderabteilung, 2 Passage, 3 Empfang und Warenausgabe, 4 Kasse, 5 Herrenabteilung, 6 Handlager, 7 Geschäftsführer, 8 Damenabteilung, 9 Kundenlift, 10 Warenaufzug, 11 Nebentreppe, 12 Haupttreppenhaus zu den Büros.

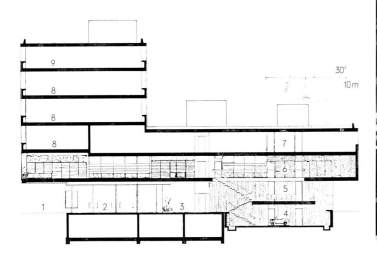

30'
10 m

6, 7. In the open entrance recess there are three low island show-cases. The usual main display window has been replaced by a plain all-glass front to give an unimpeded view of the sales area. The necessary display windows are placed on the sides of the open entrance recess.

6, 7. Die Passage vor dem Eingang. In der Zugangszone stehen nur drei niedrige Vitrinen. Auf ein frontales Schaufenster wurde zugunsten einer durchgehenden Nurglaswand verzichtet, so daß man von der Passage aus die Verkaufsräume in voller Tiefe überblicken kann. Die erforderlichen Schaufenster liegen an den Seiten, ohne die Transparenz des Gesamtraumes zu stören.

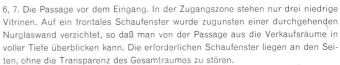

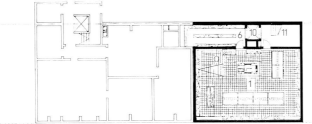

8. View from the gallery of the women's department on the first floor. The gallery links the inner and the outer sales areas. Since much of the already limited ground-floor space had to be used for the entrance display area, the remaining sales area (the children's department) was constructed at a level about 4 ft lower than the rest. A bridge-like platform (the men's department) was then built over this sunken area. From the men's department a further stairway leads to the first floor (the women's department). By this device an extra sales area was gained near the ground floor and continuity was established between the different levels. The consequent elimination of parts of the ceiling provides a large, continuous airspace which allows the storeys to be of a moderate height.

9. Wooden ceiling grid with light coffers in the children's department.

10. All three sales levels can be seen from the reception area, which leads directly into the open-fronted entrance recess. Clear glass balustrades add to the lightness of the store. The overall illumination is by means of coffer lights and spots, but a circle of white cylindrical lamps and an arrangement of spherical lights are used to provide atmosphere.

8. Blick von der Galerie der Damenabteilung im ersten Obergeschoß, die als Verbindungsbrücke zur rückwärtigen Verkaufszone dient. Da für die Schaufensterpassage ein guter Teil der ohnedies knappen Erdgeschoßfläche geopfert werden mußte, legte man die verbleibende Verkaufsfläche (Kinderabteilung) um etwa 1,20 m tiefer. Dadurch konnte über dem Tiefteil eine brückenartige Plattform (Herrenabteilung) eingezogen werden, von der aus ein weiterer Treppenlauf zum ersten Obergeschoß (Damenabteilung) hinaufführt. Auf diese Weise ließ sich nahe dem Erdgeschoß zusätzliche Verkaufsfläche gewinnen und zugleich eine offene, kontinuierliche Verbindung der Verkaufsebenen erzielen. Die Deckenaussparungen ergaben einen zusammenhängenden großen Luftraum, der mäßige Geschoßhöhen erlaubte.

9. Gitterdecke aus Holzlamellen und Leuchtkästen in der Kinderabteilung.

10. Vom Empfangsbereich auf Höhe der Schaufensterpassage aus lassen sich alle drei Verkaufsebenen überblicken. Klarglasbrüstungen steigern die Transparenz des Gesamtraumes. Eine Lichttraube aus Kugellampen und ein Radleuchter mit weißen Zylindern ergänzen als Stimmungsträger die in die Decken eingelassenen Leuchtwannen und Punktstrahler.

Book Shop in London

Architect: David Rock, London

When the oldest London book shop, John & Edward Bumpus, Ltd., moved into Berk House in Baker Street, it was necessary that the new rooms had a modern character yet still expressed the time-honoured traditions of the house. On the one hand, the books had to be stored as compactly as possible; on the other, provision had to be made for generous sitting and reading space for customers. A further sales room is situated under the front third of the shop, the street front of which occupies two building bays. To comply with strict fire requirements, a smoke vestibule separating the ground floor from the basement had to be provided; and the staircase had to lead through the vestibule to open directly on to the street. These requirements were both solved by recessing the window front along one bay.

Buchhandlung in London

Architekt: David Rock, London

Beim Umzug der ältesten Londoner Buchhandlung, der John & Edward Bumpus Ltd., in das Berk House an der Baker Street sollten die neuen Geschäftsräume ein modernes, aber doch traditionsbewußtes Gepräge erhalten. Einerseits war für eine sehr kompakte Unterbringung des Bücherangebots zu sorgen, andererseits sollten der Kundschaft reichlich Sitzplätze zum Lesen zur Verfügung gestellt werden. Unter dem vorderen Drittel des Lokals, dessen Straßenfront die Breite von zwei Gebäudeachsen einnimmt, liegt ein weiterer Verkaufsraum. Er wird über eine frei in den Raum gestellte Treppe erschlossen. Strenge feuerpolizeiliche Vorschriften machten die Einschaltung einer vestibülartigen Rauchschleuse notwendig, die das Erdgeschoß vom Untergeschoß trennt; außerdem mußte die Treppe über das Vestibül direkt ins Freie führen. Diese Auflagen wurden durch Zurücknehmen der Fensterwand in der einen Achse gelöst.

1. View from the entrance bay of the ground floor sales room leading to the vestibule on to the longitudinal passageway to the rear part of the shop: the sculpture at the end of the passage serves to arrest the eye. The columns inside the shop are treated as display units.

2–4. Longitudinal section, plans of ground floor and basement.

5. Entrance to the smoke vestibule.

6. The shop front at night.

1. Blick von dem auf das Vestibül führenden Eingang des Erdgeschoß-Verkaufsraumes auf den Längsgang zum hinteren Ladenteil, an dessen Ende eine Plastik als Blickfang plaziert ist. Die Pfeiler im Gebäudeinneren sind zu Vitrinen ausgestaltet.

2–4. Längsschnitt, Grundriß von Erdgeschoß und Untergeschoß.

5. Eingang zum Rauch-Vestibül.

6. Die Ladenfront bei Nacht.

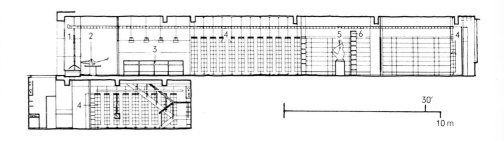

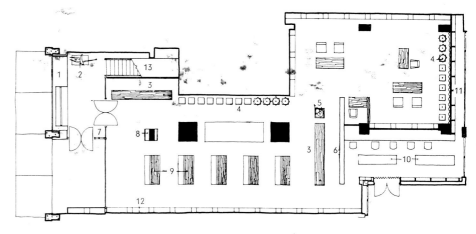

30'
10 m

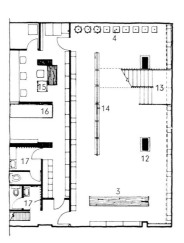

Key to the plans: 1 Display window, 2 Vestibule, 3 Counter, 4 Revolving book stacks, 5 Sculpture, 6 Partition wall, 7 Display board, 8 Show case, 9 Couches and shelves, 10 Packing tables, 11 Manual storage, 12 Shelves, 13 Staircase to the basement, 14 Display stand for greeting cards, 15 Telephone exchange, 16 Packing table, 17 W. C.

Legende zu den Plänen: 1 Schaufenster, 2 Vestibül, 3 Ladentisch, 4 Drehbare Buchständer, 5 Skulptur, 6 Trennwand, 7 Ausstellungstafel, 8 Ausstellungsvitrine, 9 Sitzbänke und Regale, 10 Packtische, 11 Handlager, 12 Regale, 13 Treppe zum Untergeschoß, 14 Ständer für Grußkarten, 15 Telefonzentrale, 16 Packtisch, 17 WC.

7. View through the main sales area towards the large floor-to-ceiling display window in the recessed entrance bay. In the foreground, the seating bays for customers. In all of the rooms, ceilings are constructed from 4 in slats of copper-plated sheet steel and hung 2 ft below the structural ceiling; they screen beams, pipes and the sprinkler system and act as louvres to the lamps installed above them. The walls are either covered with ribbed wood panels, or plastered and painted white or dark green. The floor is covered with plastic tiles.

8. The arts and architecture department adjoining the main sales room.

9. The sales room in the basement. Left, the display stand for greeting cards. In the background, the revolving book stacks installed at various points in the shop.

7. Blick durch den Hauptverkaufsraum auf das große raumhohe Schaufenster in der zurückgesetzten Eingangsbucht. Im Vordergrund die Kojen mit Sitzbänken für Kunden. Lamellendecke in sämtlichen Räumen aus 10 cm hohen, verkupferten Stahlblechstreifen, die 60 cm unter der Raumdecke hängen; sie verdecken Unterzüge, Leitungen und das Sprinklersystem und streuen das Licht der darüber befestigten Lampen. Wände teils mit gerippten Holztafeln verkleidet, teils weiß oder dunkelgrün verputzt. Fußboden Kunststoff-Fliesen.

8. Die Abteilung für Kunst und Architektur, die an den Hauptverkaufsraum anschließt.

9. Der Verkaufsraum im Untergeschoß. Links das Regal für Grußkarten. Im Hintergrund die drehbaren Buchständer, die an verschiedenen Stellen der Buchhandlung eingebaut sind.

1, 2. Window display, the walnut book stands are about 38$\frac{1}{2}$ in wide. The front section slopes by about 60°, the middle section by about 20°, the back panel can be revolved on pivots. The lower part of the stand can be pulled back on casters by about 16 in to make it accessible from the front.

1, 2. Schaufensterauslage mit den 98 cm breiten Bücherständern aus Nußbaum. Frontfläche etwa 60° geneigt, Mittelfläche etwa 20°, senkrechte Rückwand auf Zapfen drehbar. Unterer Teil auf Kugelrollen 40 cm zurückziehbar, so daß der Bücherständer von vorne zugänglich ist.

Book Shop in Milan

Architects: Luigi Figini and Gino Pollini, Milan

Buchhandlung in Mailand

Architekten: Luigi Figini und Gino Pollini, Mailand

With a floor area of about 697 sq yd (482 on the ground floor and 215 on the mezzanine) the Libreria Hoepli is one of the biggest book shops in Europe. Its success lies in its spaciousness and ease of supervision inside the shop. This is apparent in the well organized grouping of books under subjects and, on the outside, by the impressive display window about 140 ft long, where more than 1000 books can be shown at the same time. This window can be divided into sections by adjustable panels. The main sales room is glazed on three sides, and on the long inner wall a gallery was installed with wall shelves in convenient reach. The display tables on the ground floor are made up of cubical units which can be combined in any number of ways.

Mit 583 m² (403 m² ebenerdig, 180 m² im Zwischengeschoß) ist die Libreria Hoepli eine der größten europäischen Buchhandlungen. Großzügigkeit und übersichtliche Gliederung sind auch die wichtigsten Gestaltungsmerkmale. Im Inneren werden sie vor allem in der klaren Ordnung nach Sachgebieten sichtbar, im Äußeren in der imponierenden Ausstellungsfläche, die sich bei einer Schaufensterfront von 43 m Länge ergibt. Über 1000 Bücher können gleichzeitig in der Auslage gezeigt werden. Sie ist in einzelne Felder mit schräg geneigten Flächen und senkrechter Rückwand aufgelöst. An der inneren Längsseite des dreiseitig verglasten Hauptverkaufsraums wurde eine Empore eingebaut, deren Wandregale bequeme Greifhöhe haben. Die Ausstellungstische in den Verkaufsräumen des Erdgeschosses setzen sich aus kubischen Einheiten mit Regalen an den Seiten zusammen; sie können beliebig kombiniert werden.

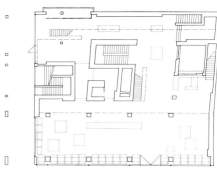

3. Detail view of the shop front on the long facade. In front of the display window, a wide arcade provides protection from the weather, the entrance is to the right. The gallery is visible over the display panels.
4. Ground floor plan.
5. View from the entrance towards the sales area under the gallery. In the background to the right, the lifts and a planted patio. Wooden book shelves varnished grey are about 7 ft high and about 12 in deep.
6. View of the rear sales room with a plant filled light well behind the window pane.
7. The main sales room seen from the gallery. Floor of white flecked granite, walls light grey, pillars of rose-coloured granite, aluminium window frames. Even lighting is achieved by additional illumination in the darker areas, e.g. by luminous beams at the front of the shop.

3. Teilansicht der Ladenfront auf der Längsseite. Vor der Schaufensterzone breite, wettergeschützte Arkade, rechts der Eingang, über den Ausstellungstafeln ist das Emporengeschoß zu erkennen.
4. Grundriß des Erdgeschosses.
5. Blick vom Eingang her auf die Verkaufsfläche unter der Empore. Rechts hinten Fahrstühle und bepflanzter Innenhof. Bücherregale aus Holz 2,2 m hoch, 30 cm tief, grau lackiert.
6. Blick in den rückwärtigen Verkaufsraum mit bepflanztem Lichtschacht hinter Glasscheibe.
7. Der Hauptverkaufsraum von der Empore aus. Fußboden weißgesprenkelter Granit, Wände helles Grau, Pfeiler rosafarbener Granit, Fensterprofile Aluminium. Gleichmäßige, da in den dunkleren Raumteilen stärkere Beleuchtung, im vorderen Ladenteil auch durch freihängende Leuchtbalken.

1, 2. Plan of ground floor and basement. Key: 1 Entrance, 2 Cashier's desk, 3 Desk, 4 Book-vending machine for after-hours service, 5 Lift, 6 Desks, 7 Wardrobe.

1, 2. Grundriß von Erdgeschoß und Untergeschoß: 1 Eingang, 2 Kasse, 3 Arbeitsplatz, 4 Buchautomat für Nachtbedienung, 5 Lift, 6 Arbeitsplätze, 7 Garderobe.

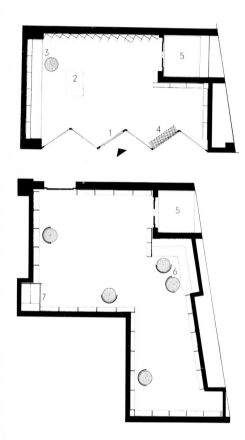

Paperback Book Shop in Berne

Architect: Hans Eichenberger,
Stuckishaus, near Berne

In answer to the rapidly growing demand for paperback books, Hanns Stauffacher, the Berne booksellers, established a branch in the Neuengasse arcade devoted exclusively to the sale of these books. A concertina-like all-glass facade affords the public ready access to bookstands stocked with recent publications, without blocking the public right of way. Passers-by can leaf through the books without coming into the shop, and the stands can be controlled from the other side of the glass front. The interior design consists virtually of the books themselves, as their standard size determines the height of the shelves. The walls of books are clearly arranged and can easily be kept under surveillance. A lift takes the customer to the basement sales area.

Taschenbuchladen in Bern

Architekt: Hans Eichenberger,
Stuckishaus bei Bern

Um der rapiden Ausweitung des Taschenbuchsortimentes Rechnung zu tragen, richtete die Berner Buchhandlung Hanns Stauffacher unter den Lauben der Neuengasse ein Zweiggeschäft ein, das ausschließlich Taschenbücher verkauft. Die in voller Höhe verglaste Fassade wurde im Zickzack gewinkelt, so daß tagsüber fahrbare Buchständer mit Neuerscheinungen auf gesetzlich statthafte Weise in der Laube aufgestellt werden können, ohne öffentliche Bodenfläche zu beanspruchen. So können Passanten in den Büchern blättern, ohne den Laden betreten zu müssen, während vom Innenraum aus durch die Glasscheiben jederzeit eine Kontrolle möglich ist. Die Inneneinrichtung tritt ganz zugunsten der Taschenbücher zurück, deren einheitliche Größe die Höhe der Regale bestimmte. Auf diese Weise entstanden klar geordnete, übersichtliche Bücherwände. Das Erdgeschoß und der Verkaufsraum im Untergeschoß sind durch einen Lift miteinander verbunden.

3. Night view. The acoustic ceiling panels extend into the arcade itself and make the shop appear larger than it actually is. Spherical lamps hang down into the angles of the zig-zag front. During the day-time these recesses house revolving bookstands. On the right one can see the side of a book-vending machine set into the glass facade.

4. View of the basement with its peaceful library-like atmosphere. In the corner on the left is a double desk. The fluorescent ceiling-light runs the whole length of the room.

5, 6. Detailed views of the arrangement of the interior. Cash register and small locker for packing material mounted on a central column. To the right, zig-zag book shelves.

3. Nachtansicht. Die in der Passage unter den Lau-ben weitergeführten Akustikplatten der Decke ver-größern optisch den Ladenraum. In den Zickzack-winkeln der Glasfassade hängen die Kugellampen in einer Linie abwechselnd vor und hinter der Glas-fläche. Die Winkel nehmen tagsüber fahrbare Buch-stånder auf. Rechts in Seitenansicht der in die Glas-front eingegliederte Buchautomat.

4. Blick in das Untergeschoß, das sich durch eine ruhige Bibliotheksatmosphäre auszeichnet. Im Winkel links der Doppelarbeitsplatz. Das Leuchtröhrenband an der Decke führt den Käufer durch den Raum.

5, 6. Detailansichten der Inneneinrichtung. Registrier-kasse und kleiner Kasten für Packmaterial sind auf einem Säulenfuß montiert. Rechts ein zickzackför-miges Bücherregal.

Book Shop in Düsseldorf

Architects: H. Brauns and R. Janeschitz-
Kriegl, Düsseldorf

The Schwan & Böger book shop on the Königsallee occupies a deep, narrow room about 14 ft high in a building which dates from the turn of the century. When the shop was redesigned, the display and storage facilities had to be improved, whilst retaining the essential intimacy of the desk arrangement. The partition wall, which had divided the room into two halves, was torn down. The resulting large, rectangular space is framed on three sides by shelves extending the full height of the room. Half way between the ceiling and the floor there is a projecting gallery. Three desks were placed in the centre of the shop, their free sides flanked by book shelves 3 ft high. The dark green colour of the ceiling makes the room appear lower. By making economical use of the space available, the shelf area was increased by 75 %.

Buchhandlung in Düsseldorf

Architekten: H. Brauns und R. Janeschitz-
Kriegl, Düsseldorf

Beim Umbau der Buchhandlung Schwan & Böger, die in einem um die Jahrhundertwende errichteten Gebäude an der Königsallee ein schmales tiefes Ladenlokal von 4,28 m lichter Höhe innehat, sollten die Ausstellungs- und Lagerungsmöglichkeiten verbessert werden, während in der Anordnung der Arbeitsplätze der bisherige intime Charakter beizubehalten war. Durch Beseitigen der Trennwand, die das Lokal in halber Tiefe unterteilte, wurde ein großer einheitlicher Raum geschaffen, den auf drei Seiten bis zur Decke reichende, raumsparend angeordnete Regale umgeben. Auf halber Höhe läuft eine in den Raum auskragende Galerie um. In der Mitte des Ladens konnten drei Arbeitsplätze in Verbindung mit 0,92 m hohen Regalschränken geschaffen werden, die auf drei Seiten wie Schutzwände um die Schreibtische herumgestellt sind. Die Höhe des Raumes wird durch die dunkelgrüne Farbgebung der Decke und die Holzbrüstung der Galerie gemildert. Die ökonomische Regalnutzung brachte eine Erhöhung der Bücherstellfläche um 75 %.

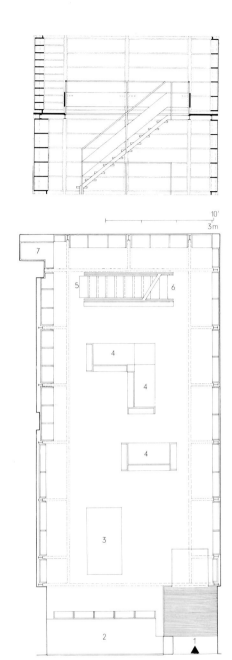

1. The books are displayed on adjustable prefabricated shelves in a self-supporting steel framework; the effect is one of order and calm. Floors covered with grey sheet p.v.c.; the ironwork painted matt black; all wooden surfaces panelled with wengé wood.

2, 3. Section and plan. Key: 1 Entrance, 2 Window display, 3 Packing table, 4 Work-desk, 5 Staircase to gallery, 6 Staircase to store-room in cellar, 7 Wardrobe. Since the thin enclosing walls were not load-bearing, the small double-T-shaped supporting pillars standing against the walls were driven through the cellar roof and anchored to the main ceiling.

4. View through the entrance. The door and the display window are framed in steel, which also serves to stiffen the framework of the shelves. As the display rack in the window is no higher than a table, the view into the store is unobstructed and the interior becomes part of the display. This is particularly apparent at night, when the fluorescent lights under the gallery and the big, spherical, free-hanging lamps are one.

1. Gesamtansicht von der Galerie. In die selbsttragende Stahlkonstruktion sind vorgefertigte Regalschränke mit verstellbaren Fachböden eingeschoben, die ein sehr ruhiges, geschlossenes Bild ergeben. Fußböden mit Bahnen aus grauem Kunststoff belegt, alles Eisenwerk mattschwarz gestrichen, alle Holzflächen mit Wengé furniert.

2, 3. Querschnitt und Grundriß. Legende: 1 Eingang, 2 Schaufensterauslage, 3 Packtisch, 4 Arbeitsplatz, 5 Treppe zur Galerie, 6 Treppe zum Lagerraum im Keller, 7 Garderobe. Da auf die dünnen Umfassungswände keine Lasten übertragen werden konnten, sind die direkt an den Wänden stehenden schmalen Doppel-T-Stützen durch die Kellerdecke geführt und oben in der Decke verankert.

4. Blick durch den Eingang. Tür und Schaufenster sind von einer Stahlkonstruktion gerahmt, die zugleich das Traggerüst der Regalwände aussteift. Da die tischhohe Bücherauslage im Schaufenster völlig freie Einsicht in den Innenraum läßt, ist dieser wirkungsvoll in die Auslage einbezogen, besonders wenn die großen weißen Kugellampen brennen.

Music and Record Shop in Vienna

Architects: Karl and Eva Mang, Vienna

When the 'Musik-Müller' shop, which had been established for more than a century, was rebuilt, the architects' brief was to create ideal conditions for the storage of such items as scores, text-books and sheet-music. To this end they designed a moderately-priced storage system that was more efficient and durable than the old method of using cardboard files. The side nearest the street was kept completely clear, but the other walls of the 290 sq ft sales-room and the 161 sq ft record department were covered from floor to ceiling with metal framing containing 750 drawers (for details see pl. 7–9). The light fittings are set in a ceiling grid in which spotlights, set into wooden cubes, alternate with light panels fitted with fluorescent tubes covered with translucent plastic sheet. Wengé wood is used throughout the shop.

Musikalien- und Schallplattengeschäft in Wien

Architekten: Karl und Eva Mang, Wien

Beim Umbau dieses schon über hundert Jahre bestehenden Geschäfts »Musik-Müller« sollten optimale Lagerbedingungen für Musikalien (Noten, Textbücher) geschaffen werden, wobei die übliche Aufbewahrung mittels drehbarer Pappdeckel durch eine dauerhaftere, ansprechende und doch preiswerte Konstruktion zu ersetzen war. Vor die Wände des von der Straße aus voll einzusehenden, rund 27 m² großen Verkaufsraums und der dahinter liegenden 15 m² großen Schallplattenabteilung wurde ein raumhohes Gerüst aus Metallprofilen gesetzt, das insgesamt 750 Schubkasteneinheiten aufnimmt (Details siehe Abb. 7–9). Die Beleuchtung ist in eine kubische Rasterdecke eingebaut, bei der Punktstrahler in Massivholzquadraten mit tiefer liegenden Leuchtfeldern (Leuchtstoffröhren mit Kunststoffolie überspannt) wechseln. Alle Holzteile bestehen aus Wengé.

1. Overall view from Krügerstraße. The all-glass entrance is on extreme left of the facade. The exterior of the shop-front is framed with dark grey slate. Four tables on castors serve as display units. Above them, a brass grid with spotlights. The window end of the right wall is faced with dark blue glazed tiles in three different sizes; it conceals an electric storage-heater. There is a frieze of red glazed tiles above the passage to the record department. Grey wall-to-wall carpeting.

2. Floor plan. Key: 1 Music sales-room, 2 Record sales-room, 3 Staff room, 4 Listening booth, 5 Storage heater, 6 Counter, 7 Record bar.

3–5. Interspersed among the banks of drawers containing sheet music are recesses with shelves for storing text-books, pocket scores, etc. The insides of the doors are also used as shelves. Below them, tables on castors for the sale of records.

1. Gesamtansicht von der Krügerstraße aus. Eingang als Ganzglaskonstruktion übereck. Glasfläche außen mit dunkelgrauem Spaltschiefer umrahmt. Auslage aus vier Rolltischen bestehend, darüber Beleuchtungskasten in Messing für Punktleuchten. Rechte Fensterwand aus dunkelblau glasierten Tonplatten in drei Größen zur Verkleidung des elektrischen Nachtspeicherofens. Rot glasierte Tonplatten als Fries über dem Durchgang zur Schallplattenabteilung. Fußboden grauer Spannteppich.

2. Grundriß. Legende: 1 Verkaufsraum für Musikalien, 2 Verkaufsraum für Schallplatten, 3 Personalraum, 4 Abhörkabine, 5 Nachtspeicherofen, 6 Verkaufstisch, 7 Phonobar.

3–5. Zwischen den Wandfächern sind Regalnischen zur Aufbewahrung von Textbüchern, Taschenpartituren usw. ausgespart. Die Innenseiten der Türen dienen ebenfalls als Regale. Darunter finden Rolltische zum Plattenverkauf Platz. Einzelne Wände mit horizontaler Holzschalung, in deren Nutung Drahtbügel als Plattenhalter eingehängt werden.

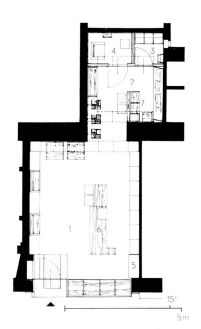

15'
5m

6. The record bar in the record department, showing how the grooves in the horizontal wood panelling are used to hold record display mounts.

7–9. The sheet music lies in piles on plywood boards which can be pushed in and out of the metal framework at will. The framework itself is composed of long flat strips, with short L-shaped sections to act as runners. Each compartment has a hinged flap made of ⅛ in hardboard veneered with wengé wood. The flaps are brass-edged along the base and have brass label-holders. They can be lifted by means of a slot, and they can be made to stay open by placing them under the flaps of the compartments above.

6. An der Wand neben der Phonobar können neue Platten auf abnehmbaren Drahtbügeln oder in kleinen Blechtrögen ausgestellt werden.

7–9. In die Gestelle aus Winkel- und Flacheisen werden die Noten auf Sperrholzplatten eingeschoben, die an einer Griffleiste herauszuziehen sind. Verschluß der Fächer durch Klappdeckel aus 4 mm starken Hartfaserplatten mit Wengéfurnier und Messingkante sowie Messingschild für auswechselbare Beschriftung. Der Deckel kann mit Hilfe einer Aussparung im Schild aufgeklappt, nach oben geschwenkt und unter den Deckel des darüberliegenden Faches geklemmt werden.

1. View from the side of the stairway along the underside of the gallery which, in the same way as the horizontally braced upright framing, compensates for the extreme height of the room. In the rear, right, between two vertical blinds, the till.
2. View through the entrance. Lighting mainly by adjustable spotlights. In the rear, latticework with adjustable brackets with the gallery in front of it.

1. Blick von der Seite des Treppenaufgangs in Längsrichtung unter der Galerie entlang, die zusammen mit den senkrecht stehenden, horizontal gespannten Rahmenbrettern die extreme Raumhöhe mildert. Rechts hinten zwischen zwei Vertikalblenden die Kasse.
2. Blick durch den Eingang. Beleuchtung vorwiegend mit verstellbaren Punktstrahlern. Im Hintergrund Gitterwand mit verstellbaren Konsolborden, davor die Galerie.

Radio and Television Shop in Milan

Architect: Pierluigi Spadolini, Florence

Radio- und Schallplattengeschäft in Mailand

Architekt: Pierluigi Spadolini, Florenz

Three display windows of the sales rooms of Messrs. Radiomarelli face on to the Galleria Vittorio Emanuele. They occupy two storeys, each of which is of about 102 sq yds. The ground floor serves as exhibition area for radio and television sets, while the upper storey contains the record department and the office rooms. The ground floor is unusually high and the front pillars are remarkably large (about 4 ft across). Inside the shop, there is a pair of cast iron columns. In order to subdivide the height of the room, a bridge-like gallery was constructed which serves also as a landing to the stairway. The overall impression of the room is established by the wood latticework wall panelling and by the fixed and movable wall boards, which can be used to create interesting spatial effects. Brackets to carry objects on display are suspended from the latticework panels.

Die Verkaufsräume der Firma Radiomarelli gehen mit drei Schaufenstern auf die Galleria Vittorio Emanuele. Sie nehmen zwei Stockwerke von je 85 m² ein, wobei das Erdgeschoß als Ausstellungsraum für Radio- und Fernsehgeräte dient, während das Obergeschoß die Schallplattenabteilung und Büroräume aufnimmt. Der ebenerdige Raum zeigt eine ungewohnte Höhe und Frontpfeiler von beträchtlicher Stärke (1,20 m). Im Inneren steht ein Paar gußeiserne Säulen. Um die Raumhöhe zu unterteilen, wurde eine brückenartige Galerie eingezogen, die zugleich als Treppenpodest für den Aufgang zum Obergeschoß dient. Der Raumeindruck wird bestimmt durch die Wandverkleidung aus Holzgittern, in deren Leisten Konsolen für das Ausstellungsgut eingehängt werden können, und durch feste oder bewegliche Wandtafeln, die interessante räumliche Effekte ermöglichen.

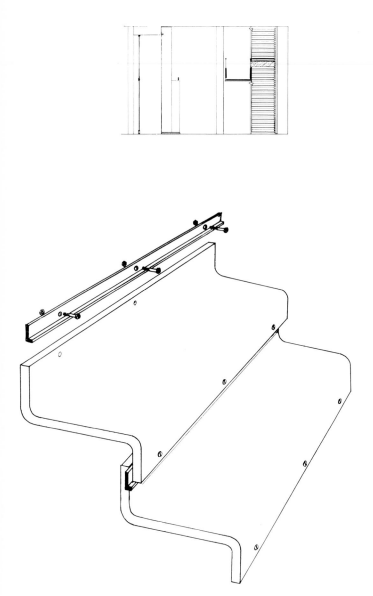

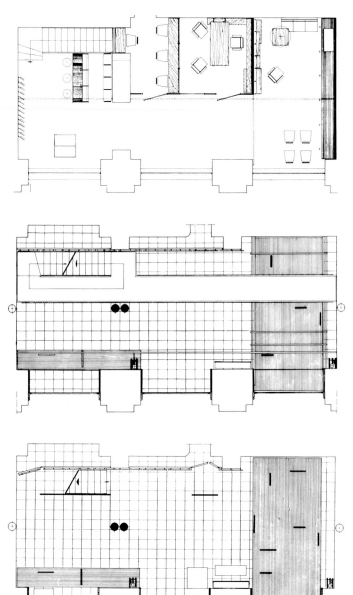

3. Section of ground floor, gallery, stairway to the upper floor.

4–6. Plans of upper floor (above), gallery and ground floor.

7. Perspective drawing of the stairway with stairs of plywood.

8, 9. Section and view of the U-shaped plywood beam under the gallery bridge. Key: 1 Transversally stressed metal profile, 2 Floor of teak strips, 3 Tension member of the suspension at the balustrade.

3. Querschnitt von Erdgeschoß, Galerie, Treppe zum Obergeschoß.

4–6. Grundrisse von Obergeschoß (oben), Galerie und Erdgeschoß.

7. Perspektive der Treppe aus Schichtholzstufen.

8, 9. Querschnitt und Ansicht der U-förmigen Schichtholzträger unter der Galeriebrücke. Legende: 1 Quergespanntes Metallprofil, 2 Fußboden aus Teakholzriemen, 3 Zugstab der Aufhängung an der Brüstung.

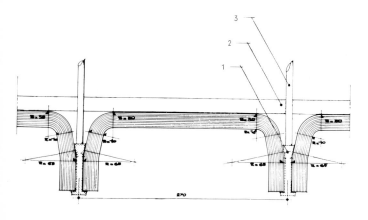

10. Long view down between the display window front and the entrance to the right and the gallery on the left. Teak panels form display islands on the marble floor.

11. View along the underside of the gallery and the stairway to the upper floor. Behind the glass balustrade, right above, the second stairway which leads from the gallery up to the record department is visible. Right, the lattice wall with adjustable glass shelves of different widths and depths which are keyed into the latticework.

12. Movable and fixed wall boards at half and full ceiling height define the different areas. Under the upright solid cheek of the balustrade, the tension rods are visible on which the U-shaped plywood sections of the bridge are mounted.

10. Längsblick zwischen Schaufensterfront mit Eingang rechts und Galerie links. Bodenplatten aus Teakholz heben auf dem Marmorfußboden Ausstellungsinseln heraus.

11. Blick unter der Galerie entlang auf die Treppe zum Obergeschoß. Rechts oben ist hinter der Glasbrüstung der zweite Treppenzug zu erkennen, der von der Galerie zur Schallplattenabteilung hinaufführt. Rechts die Lattenwand mit verstellbaren, verschieden breiten und tiefen Konsoltablaren, die zwischen das Sprossenwerk eingeklemmt werden.

12. Bewegliche und feststehende Wandtafeln in halber und voller Raumhöhe markieren Raumteile. Unter der senkrecht stehenden massiven Brüstungswange der Galerie sind die Zugstäbe zu erkennen, an denen die U-förmigen Schichtholzprofile der Brücke aufgehängt sind.

Radio and Television Shop in Hanover

Architect: Anton G. Bee, Oberwil,
Switzerland

The modern extension built onto the Mitteldorf radio shop on the Friedrichswall is used chiefly to display radio and television sets. Each item is plugged into the electrical supply and ready for use. The rear part of the shop contains the record department. In order to make it possible for people in both areas to listen to music at the same time without being disturbed, the listening-booths were planned as room-dividers down the longitudinal axis. However, to preserve the visual continuity between the record department and the rest of the main room, the fronts and the backs of the booths were made entirely of glass. The lights and the amplifiers are housed in the ceiling grid of the booths. An air-conditioning plant and a smoke extractor ensure continuous fresh air in the individual booths the back walls of which are screened off at eye-level with enlargements of photographs.

Radio- und Fernsehgeschäft in Hannover

Architekt: Anton G. Bee, Oberwil, Schweiz

Der moderne Anbau des Radiogeschäfts Mitteldorf am Friedrichswall ist zum überwiegenden Teil der Ausstellung von Fernseh- und Rundfunkgeräten vorbehalten, wobei jeder Apparat betriebsbereit angeschlossen ist. Der hintere Teil des Ladens nimmt das Schallplattenstudio auf. Damit in beiden Bereichen gleichzeitig ungestört Musik gehört werden kann, wurden die Schallplatten-Abhörkabinen als Raumteiler quer zur Längsachse eingebaut. Um das Plattenstudio optisch aber doch mit dem Hauptraum zu verbinden, wurde die Tür- und Rückseite der Kabinen vom Boden bis zur Decke verglast. Die Beleuchtung und die Lautsprecher sind in das Deckenraster der Kabinen eingebaut. Eine Klimaanlage mit zusätzlicher Rauchabzugsvorrichtung sorgt für ständigen Luftwechsel in den einzelnen Kabinen, deren Rückseite in Blickhöhe Phototafeln als Sichtblenden trägt.

1. View from the front of the showroom looking towards the listening-booths with the record department behind them. False ceiling of plaster with built-in recessed lights. Walls papered and painted matt white or partially faced with natural wood. The front of the pillar is fitted with a wooden fascia concealing fluorescent lights, wall-to-wall carpets.
2. View of the listening-booths from the record bar, most of which is covered with white plastic panels.
3. Detail of one of the record bar turn-tables. Display shelves with wooden sides and glass carriers.
4. In front of the walnut-veneered side wall, a counter with troughs to hold records.

1. Blick aus dem vorderen Ausstellungsraum auf die querstehenden Abhörkabinen, dahinter die Schallplattenabteilung. Hängedecke aus Gips mit eingebauten Tiefstrahlern. Wände tapeziert und mit Dispersionsfarbe mattweiß gestrichen. Teilweise Naturholzverschalung. Einseitige Pfeilerverkleidungen mit Holzblenden vor Leuchtstoffröhren. Bodenbelag Spannteppich.
2. Blick über die Schallplattenbar, deren Kasten mit weißen Kunststoffplatten verkleidet ist, auf die Abhörkabinen.
3. Detailansicht des Abspieltisches und der Plattenbar. Regal mit Seitenwänden aus Holz und Glastablaren.
4. Vor der nußbaumfurnierten Seitenwand der Schallplattenabteilung ein Konsolentisch mit trogförmigen Vertiefungen für Platten.

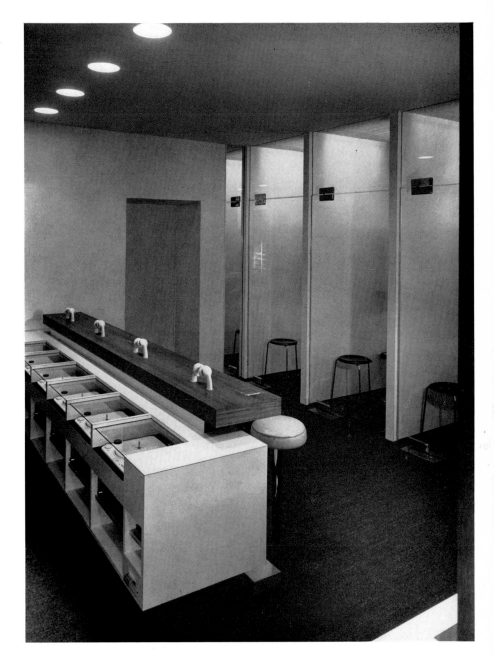

Branch Store of a Swiss Sewing Machine
Company in Vienna

Architect: Carl Auböck, Vienna

A relatively small old shop, on the corner of Stephansplatz and Jasomirgottgasse in Vienna, had to be redesigned to provide sufficient room for the demonstration and sale of sewing machines, as well as two offices, display areas and storage units for accessories and sewing materials. The upper parts of the partition walls were already glazed, so when it came to dividing the shop into its component areas, coloured screens with advertising slogans were fixed at eye level to those areas that had to be closed off; for the rest, the glass remained. In this way the required visual and acoustical insulation of the various areas was obtained without destroying the overall impression of a large continuous space. The furniture and the fittings are of light-coloured larch wood. Apart from various shades of grey, only primary colours – blue, yellow and red – were used.

Niederlassung einer schweizerischen Näh-
maschinenfabrik in Wien

Architekt: Carl Auböck, Wien

Auf der verhältnismäßig kleinen Grundfläche eines Ecklokals im Stadtzentrum am Stephansplatz sollte durch Umbau ausreichender Platz für Vorführung und Verkauf von Elna-Nähmaschinen sowie für zwei Büroräume geschaffen werden; ferner waren Auslageflächen und ein Handlager für Zubehör (Garne, Nadeln usw.) unterzubringen. Die geforderte räumliche Trennung der einzelnen Betriebsfunktionen wurde in der Weise erreicht, daß die im Oberteil verglasten Trennwände in Blickhöhe entweder mit farbigen Sichtblenden geschlossen wurden, die Werbetexte tragen, oder ebenfalls verglast sind. So konnte die gewünschte Sicht- und Schallabschirmung der einzelnen Räume untereinander erreicht werden, ohne den Eindruck eines zusammenhängenden Gesamtraumes zu stören. Außer Grautönen von Weiß bis Schwarz sind die reinen Grundfarben Blau, Gelb und Rot verwendet.

1–3. Exterior views. The small illustrations show the
two display windows on the long side, facing Jasomirgottgasse; the larger photograph shows the
view from Stephansplatz. White silhouettes of
sewing accessories painted on glass panels, hung
in the windows, indicate what the shop sells.
4. Floor plan. Key: 1 Demonstration, 2 Trials, 3 Sales,
4 Sales manager's office, 5 Office, 6 Washroom.
5. Sales room. Eye-level screens with graphics, photographs and advertising slogans.
6. Demonstration tables in the sales room.
7. The window display units consist simply of glass
or wooden shelves, fixed at the required height in a
slotted angle framework.

1–3. Außenansichten. Die kleinen Abbildungen zeigen die beiden Schaufenster auf der Längsseite an
der Jasomirgottgasse; die große Abbildung gibt die
Ansicht vom Stephansplatz wieder. Weiße Silhouetten von Nähutensilien (auf Glasplatten gemalt und
ins Schaufenster gehängt) signalisieren die Art des
Ladens.
4. Grundriß: 1 Vorführung, 2 Einschulung, 3 Verkauf,
4 Büro Verkaufsleitung, 5 Büro, 6 WC/Waschraum.
5. Verkaufsraum. In Blickhöhe Sichtblenden mit
Graphik, Photo und Werbetext.
6. Vorführtische im Verkaufsraum.
7. Die Auslageflächen der Schaufenster bestehen
aus leicht demontierbaren Lochschienen mit Holz-
und Glasborden.

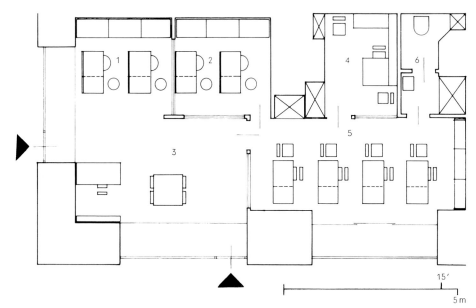

15'

5 m

1. View from the lobby through the display window. The room appears bigger because its flowing space is unbroken by rigid divisions. The hexagon motif is apparent throughout. The partition wall separating the customers' area from the workshop is composed of alternate panels of wood and brilliantly coloured shiny plastic.

2. View from the lobby entrance. Mirrors add to the illusion of flowing space. The hexagonal shape of the counter is especially space-saving. There is ample room for a customer on each of the three sides, yet the area taken up is less than with a rectangular counter.

1. Blick von der Lobby aus durch das Schaufenster. Optische Weiträumigkeit durch Verunklären der Raumgrenzen. Vom Bodenbelag bis zu den Deckenausschnitten ist das Sechseck die bestimmende Form. Die Trennwände, die den Kundenbereich von der Werkstatt trennen, tragen abwechselnd Holzfurniere und starkfarbige Kunststoffbeläge.

2. Blick vom Lobby-Eingang aus. Einzelne Spiegelflächen steigern die Illusion der Weitläufigkeit. Die Sechseckform wirkt sich beim Ladentisch besonders raumsparend aus: Obwohl der Kunde unbeengt an einer der Seiten steht, ist die Fläche geringer als bei rechteckiger Tischplatte.

Electric Shaver Service Center in New York

Architect: Gerald Luss, Designs for Business Inc., New York

The Norelco Electric Shaver Service Center provides an ideal example of how a relatively small room can be apparently enlarged by means of imaginative interior design. The service center, a longish rectangle only 880 sq ft in area, is situated on the ground floor of a building on 41st Street, from which a narrow corridor leads into the shop. There is a second entrance in the lobby of the main building, from which one can look into the interior through a display window. The design is based on a hexagon motif, which appears in the floor pattern and in the shape of the partitions, counters, lighting fixtures and seats. The resulting interaction of planes is heightened by the use of strong colours: purple, light red, black, white and various shades of blue and grey.

Service Center für Elektro-Rasierapparate in New York

Architekt: Gerald Luss, Designs for Business, Inc., New York

Das Norelco Electric Shaver Service Center ist ein Beispiel dafür, wie sich ein verhältnismäßig kleiner Raum durch einfallsreichen Innenausbau und durch Verschleiern seiner »Schachtel«-Form optisch vergrößern läßt. Das nur rund 75 m² große Lokal in Form eines langgestreckten Rechtecks liegt im Erdgeschoß eines Gebäudes an der 41. Straße, von der ein schmaler Verbindungsflur in das Geschäft führt. Ein zweiter Eingang befindet sich in der Lobby des Hauses, von der aus man durch ein Schaufenster in das Innere sehen kann. Der Entwurf basiert auf dem Motiv des Sechsecks, das als Muster im Bodenbelag erscheint und die Form der Trennwände, Ladentische, Leuchtkörper und Sitzbänke bis zum Aschbecher bestimmt. Dadurch ergeben sich vielfältige Überschneidungen und Flächenkontraste, die durch kräftige Farben – Purpur, Hellrot, Schwarz, Weiß und verschiedene Blau- und Grautöne – noch gesteigert werden.

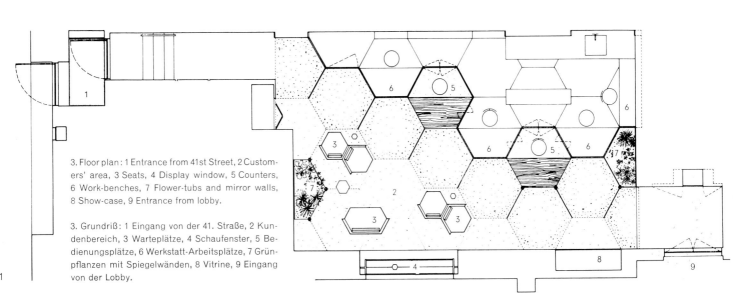

3. Floor plan: 1 Entrance from 41st Street, 2 Customers' area, 3 Seats, 4 Display window, 5 Counters, 6 Work-benches, 7 Flower-tubs and mirror walls, 8 Show-case, 9 Entrance from lobby.

3. Grundriß: 1 Eingang von der 41. Straße, 2 Kundenbereich, 3 Warteplätze, 4 Schaufenster, 5 Bedienungsplätze, 6 Werkstatt-Arbeitsplätze, 7 Grünpflanzen mit Spiegelwänden, 8 Vitrine, 9 Eingang von der Lobby.

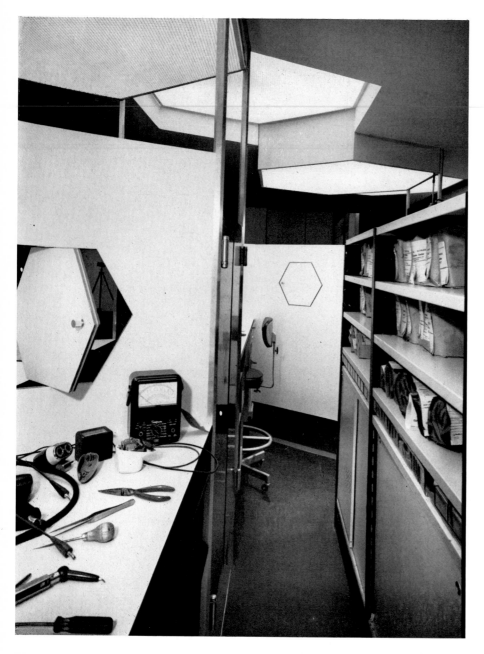

4. View of the work-benches. The hexagonal shape once again saves space, because the repair areas which jut out into the customers' area can be dovetailed with the service areas. Hexagonal hatches connect the two. The repair areas can easily be recognized from their lower ceiling lights.

5. At the entrance on 41st Street the hexagon motif is used again. Instead of a display window, there is a wall of marble slabs with a vertical line of 3 small recessed hexagonal show-cases and alternatively recessed and protruding marble hexagons.

6. Built-in show-case near the lobby entrance.

4. Blick in die Werkstatt. Der Sechseckgrundriß erweist sich als raumsparend bei der Verzahnung der beiden außerhalb der Trennwand im Kundenbereich liegenden Bedienungsplätze (im Sechseck-»Käfig« links Mitte und rechts hinten; beide mit heruntergezogener Leuchtdecke) und der vier Werkstatt-Arbeitsplätze. Durchreichen mit sechseckigen Drehklappen verbinden die Werkstatt- und Bedienungsplätze.

5. Am Eingang an der 41. Straße klingt bereits das Sechseckmotiv an. Statt eines Schaufensters ist eine Wand aus Marmorplatten eingezogen, in die drei kleine Sechseckvitrinen eingelassen wurden. Weitere Marmor-Sechsecke, die als Mulde ausgehoben oder aufgesetzt sind, vervollständigen die Reihe. Daneben der Firmenname in großen Metallbuchstaben.

6. Einbauvitrine im Vorraum des Lobbyeingangs.

Olivetti Showroom in Paris

Architects: Franco Albini and Franca Helg, Milan

Like all other Olivetti establishments, these showrooms on the Rue du Faubourg St Honoré were designed with great elegance. The square main room, with its frontage composed almost entirely of two enormous glass display windows, is linked to the inner offices by two smaller rooms, which are used for demonstration purposes. Materials and colours are the same throughout: the walls and ceilings are covered with green linen and the floor has fitted carpets of a matching shade. In the main room one's attention is immediately caught by the lattice of vertical struts, wires and wooden display shelves set at different heights. The modular system of the shelving, based on an equilateral triangle, is given additional apparent depth by the use of mirror walls.

Ausstellungsraum für Olivetti-Büromaschinen in Paris

Architekten: Franco Albini und Franca Helg, Mailand

Wie die übrigen Olivetti-Niederlassungen so wurden auch diese Räume an der Rue du Faubourg St. Honoré mit außergewöhnlicher Sorgfalt ausgestattet. Den nahezu quadratischen Hauptraum, der mit zwei geschoßhohen Schaufenstern zur Straße orientiert ist, verbinden zwei kleinere Vorführräume mit den nach rückwärts gelegenen Büros. Alle Räume wurden in Material und Farbgebung einheitlich gestaltet: Wände und Decken sind mit grünem Leinen ausgeschlagen; der Fußboden trägt einen farblich dazu passenden Spannteppich. Den Blickfang des Hauptraums bildet eine Gitterstruktur aus filigranen, polierten Mahagoni-Vertikalstreben, zwischen denen als Exponatträger in verschiedenen Höhen ebenfalls grün bespannte Holzplatten hängen. Ihre Grundform, ein gleichseitiges Dreieck, ergibt in der Addition ein räumliches Modulsystem, dessen optische Durchdringungen noch durch Spiegelwände vervielfältigt werden.

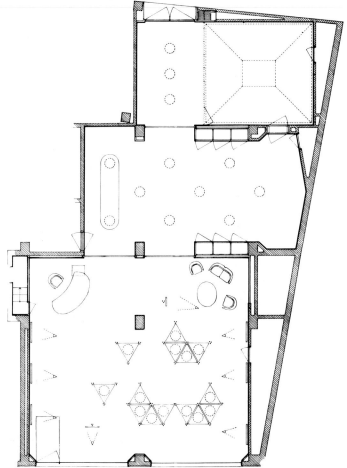

1. (Page 63) The display shelves. Lamps suspended from wires.
2. Detail of the display shelves. Round supporting struts of polished mahogany; brass fittings; shelves covered with green linen.
3. Floor plan of main area and demonstration rooms.
4. View from the street. The supports are kept in position by tensioned wires fastened to a steel frame.
5. The main lights, with their shallow glass shades (designed by the architects) form a secondary horizontal element.

1. (Seite 63) Gitterstruktur aus Stützen, Spanndrähten, eingehängten Lampen und Dreieckstafeln.
2. Detailansicht der Ausstellungsgestelle. Stützen aus polierten Mahagoni-Rundstäben, Beschläge aus Messing, dreieckige Ausstellungsflächen mit grünem Leinen bespannt.
3. Grundriß von Hauptraum und Vorführräumen.
4. Ansicht von der Straße. Die Stützen werden durch Spanndrähte gehalten, die an einem Rahmen aus Profileisen befestigt sind.
5. Flache Glasglocken runder Lampen (Architektenentwurf) bilden eine zweite Horizontale.

1, 2. The focal points are the typewriters and calculating machines exhibited in Plexiglas spheres. These have iron pedestals, which can be set in various positions by means of the sockets provided in the floor.

1, 2. Hauptblickpunkte bilden die Maschinen in Plexiglaskugeln, deren Eisenständer in Fußbodenlöchern versetzbar sind.

Showroom of Messrs. Hispano-Olivetti in Barcelona

Architects: Studio Architetti BBPR (Lodovico B. Belgiojoso, Enrico Peressutti, Ernesto N. Rogers), Milan
Assistant: José Soteras Mauri

Ausstellungsraum der Hispano-Olivetti in Barcelona

Architekten: Studio Architetti BBPR (Lodovico B. Belgiojoso, Enrico Peressutti, Ernesto N. Rogers), Mailand
Mitarbeiter: José Soteras Mauri

This showroom and sales room for typewriters and calculating machines on the ground floor of the office building which the Spanish branch of Messrs. Olivetti built in the Ronda de la Universidad in Barcelona. It was necessary for it to attract attention but in an appropriately dignified way and to combine a feeling of great spaciousness with elegance. This was achieved by making the front part two storeys high, providing it with an all-glass front, accentuating the ceiling area with clusters of large circular light fittings of varying dimensions, and finally, by making the showroom area about 60 feet wide. This impression is further emphasized by the rich materials used: grey quarzite for the floor (continued into the sidewalk), pink granite for the wall panelling, a facing of gold foil on the panels of the cantilevered ceiling, and a blue finished metal frame for the window front.

Dieser Ausstellungs- und Verkaufsraum für Schreib- und Rechenmaschinen wurde im Erdgeschoß des Bürogebäudes eingerichtet, das die spanische Olivetti-Tochtergesellschaft an der Ronda de la Universidad im Geschäftszentrum Barcelonas erbaute. Er sollte auf ebenso souveräne wie diskrete Weise Aufmerksamkeit erregen und Großzügigkeit mit Eleganz verbinden. Dies wurde einmal erreicht durch die Zweigeschossigkeit des vorderen Raumteils, der – in voller Höhe verglast und in der Deckenzone durch Bündel aus verschieden großen runden Leuchten akzentuiert – mit 18 m Breite sehr licht und weiträumig wirkt. Zweitens tragen dazu die noblen Materialien bei: grauer Quarzit für den Fußboden (auch auf dem Bürgersteig), rosafarbene Granitplatten als Wandverkleidung, Goldfolienbeschichtung auf den Feldern der auskragenden Decke und schließlich die blau lackierte Metallkonstruktion der Fensterfront.

Showroom of the Recordak Corporation for Micro-film Equipment in New York

Architects: The Space Design Group, Inc., New York 18, N.Y.

This showroom in the Sperry Rand Building on the Avenue of the Americas is characterized by the counterplay of the acoustic ceiling with its suspended sculptured blocks, and the table blocks, 30 in high, on which the micro-film systems are exhibited. One enters the showroom at street level and descends four steps into an area some 2 ft 6 in below, into which extend from the right and left the block-shaped display platforms. The floor on both levels, as well as the floor blocks, are covered with square white ceramic tiles. Clear Plexiglas sheets resting on white plastic boxes raise the apparatus above the display platforms. The continuity of the sculptured ceiling with its blocks of varying shape is interrupted by the recesses of the light wells and by slots for the distribution of conditioned air.

Ausstellungsraum der Recordak Corporation für Mikrofilm-Zubehör in New York

Architekten: The Space Design Group, Inc., New York 18, N.Y.

Dieser Ausstellungsraum im Sperry Rand Building an der Avenue of the Americas ist gekennzeichnet durch die Kontrapunktik zwischen der blockartig gegliederten Akustikdecke und den rund 75 cm hohen Tischblöcken, auf denen die Mikrofilmgeräte ausgestellt werden. Man betritt den Raum auf Straßenniveau und steigt dann über vier Stufen zum 75 cm tiefer liegenden Niveau des Innenraums hinunter, in den von rechts und links die blockförmigen Ausstellungsplattenformen hineinragen. Die Fußböden beider Niveaus und die Blöcke sind mit quadratischen weißen Keramikplättchen verkleidet. Glasklare Platten aus Kunststoff, die auf weiße Kunststoffkästen aufgelegt wurden, heben die Geräte von den Plattformen ab. Die plastisch gestaltete Decke mit ihren verschieden geformten Blöcken ist von Leuchtschächten und Öffnungen für die Klimaanlage durchbrochen.

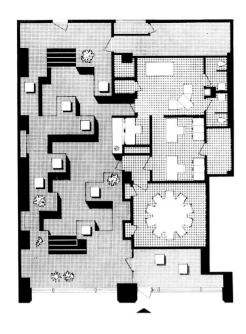

1. View from the street into the interior. The rear wall clad with bright red felt, the side walls surfaced alternatively with white felt, charcoal grey paint and sprayed cork granules painted tan.
2. Plan. Office and conferencerooms adjoining the showroom on the same level.
3. View through the showroom towards the entrance.
4. Perspective drawing of ceiling and floor.
5. The blocks of the display platforms.

1. Einblick von der Straße aus. Rückwand mit leuchtend rotem Filz bespannt, Seitenwände abwechselnd weißer Filz, anthrazitgrauer Anstrich und Auflage aus aufgespritzten, braun gestrichenen Korkpartikeln.
2. Grundriß. An den Ausstellungsraum schließen auf gleichem Niveau Büro- und Besprechungsräume an.
3. Blick durch den Raum zum Eingang.
4. Perspektive von Decke und Boden.
5. Die Blöcke der Ausstellungsplattformen.

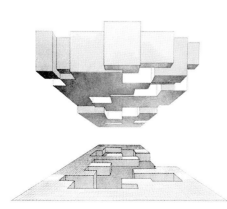

Showroom of the Xerox Corporation in New York

Architects: Eliot Noyes & Associates, New Canaan, Conn.

The space at the architects' disposal on the ground floor of the Sperry Rand Building measured 92 ft by 47 ft. Influenced by the building's large structural columns, the architects divided this area into four rectangles of about equal size: a reception area and three display areas. The latter were designed as three raised islands, with the centre one set out of line with the other two, and all of them connected by bridges. These islands, which are faced with white terrazzo, are exactly matched in shape and size by the white canopies suspended over them. The rest of the room is in neutral greys and blacks. The items on display, duplicating machines of two different sizes, stand out in sharp contrast against their surroundings through their vivid colours: yellow, orange, red and blue. Their bases have been designed to relate to the overall architectural theme.

Ausstellungsraum der Xerox Corporation in New York

Architekt: Eliot Noyes & Associates, New Canaan, Conn.

Die im Erdgeschoß des Sperry Rand Building zur Verfügung stehende Fläche von rund 28 × 14 m wurde – unter Berücksichtigung der kräftigen Rundstützen – in vier ungefähr gleich große, lang-gestreckte Felder unterteilt: eine Empfangszone und drei Ausstellungsbereiche. Diese bestehen aus drei etwas vom Boden abgehobenen und gegeneinander versetzten Inseln, die untereinander durch Brücken verbunden sind. Den mit weißem Terrazzo belegten Inseln entsprechen genau gleich ge-formte, ebenfalls weiße Baldachine, die von der Decke abgehängt wurden. Alle übrigen Teile des Raumes sind in neutralem Grau oder Schwarz gehalten. Die Ausstellungsobjekte, Kopierautomaten in zwei verschiedenen Größen, heben sich durch leuchtende Signalfarben – gelb, orange, rot und blau – von ihrer Umgebung ab. Ihre Podeste sind ebenso wie die Sockel der Bänke genau auf die Architektur abgestimmt.

1. View from the rear island, showing the central display platform. In the background are windows which run the length of the reception area.
2. View from the reception area looking towards the three raised display islands. The indentations in the canopies correspond to the connecting bridges.
3, 4. Cross-section and floor plan.
5. Night view of the main front looking towards the three islands. On the right, the revolving-door of the reception area.

1. Blick von der dritten Insel auf die zurückgesetzte mittlere und die wieder weiter vorgezogene dritte Ausstellungsplattform. Im Hintergrund die Fenster auf der Längsseite der Empfangszone.
2. Blick von der Empfangszone auf die drei höher gelegenen Ausstellungsinseln, in deren Deckenbaldachinen die Verbindungsbrücken durch Kerben markiert sind.
3, 4. Schnitt und Grundriß.
5. Nachtansicht der Hauptfront mit den drei Inseln. Rechts Drehtür zur Empfangszone.

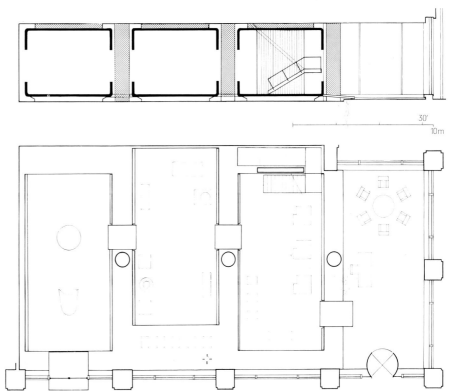

30'
10m

6. Reception area. Twin spotlights fitted flush with the plan ceiling. Beige woollen carpet.

7. The island nearest the reception area, as seen from the stairs to the second-floor offices. Large vertical blinds can be drawn over the windows. Terrazzo floor with heating ducts. The cruciform bases and pedestals were designed by Eliot Noyes.

8. The central island. Lighting: spotlights flush with the ceiling and fluorescent light panels in the canopies.

9. Bridge to the third island showing the turned-up ends of the base and the canopy.

10. Cross-section through the base and canopy of a display island. The base stands 1 ft 5 in from the floor and consists of a steel frame covered with wire-reinforced plaster, painted with white protective

paint on the outside, and faced with white terrazzo in the inside.

11. The third island, with a model mounted between panes of Plexiglas for demonstration purposes. The floor in the foreground is of unglazed black ceramic tiles. To improve the acoustics of the room, the walls are covered with charcoal-coloured tweed.

6. Die Empfangszone, deren etwas erhöhte Bodenplatte mit einem sandfarbenen Spannteppich bezogen ist. Flachdecke mit paarweise eingesetzten, bündig abschließenden Deckenstrahlern.

7. Die vorderste Insel neben dem Empfang, von der Treppe zum Büro-Zwischengeschoß aus gesehen. Die Fensterfront ist durch vertikale Lamellenstores geschlossen. Terrazzofußboden mit Heizungsschlit-

zen. Kreuzförmige Podeste Entwurf: Eliot Noyes.

8. Die zurückgesetzte mittlere Insel. Beleuchtung durch deckenbündige Punktstrahler und Leuchtfelder in den Baldachinen.

9. Brücke zur dritten Insel. Basis und Baldachin mit aufgebogenen Seitenwangen.

10. Querschnitt durch Basis und Baldachin einer Ausstellungsinsel. Basisschale, 43 cm vom Fußboden abgehoben, Stahlrahmen mit Maschendraht, außen mit Gipsputz und weißem Schutzanstrich, innen weißer Terrazzobelag.

11. Die dritte Insel mit einem zwischen Plexiglasscheiben befestigten Demonstrationsmodell. Im Vordergrund der Fußboden aus mattem schwarzem Keramikmosaik. Wände zur Verbesserung der Akustik mit anthrazitfarbenem Tweed bespannt.

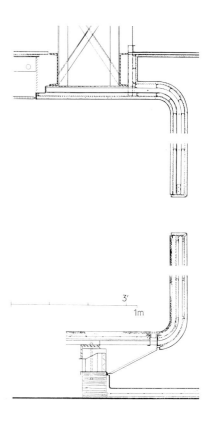

3'

1m

The showroom on the ground floor of the IBM Office Products Division Headquarters on Madison Avenue occupies a large, rectangular area, which is divided along the street front and the longitudinal axis of the room by large supporting pillars placed at regular intervals. A false ceiling composed of light panels illuminates the display area evenly, and the passer-by has an unobstructed view of the showroom through five windows on the long side and three on the short. The whole showroom is virtually one big display window and, for this reason, the designers concentrated their efforts on the window area; the aim being to convey to laymen in purely visual terms the essentially abstract and highly complex developments in computer technology.

The IBM Computer Equipment Showroom in New York

Semi-permanent exhibitions: Ward & Saks, Inc., New York

Ausstellungsraum für elektronische Datenverarbeitungsanlagen der IBM in New York

Gestaltung der Wechselausstellungen: Ward & Saks, Inc., New York

Der Ausstellungsraum im Erdgeschoß des IBM Office Products Division Headquarters an der Madison Avenue nimmt eine langgestreckte, rechteckige Grundfläche ein, die sowohl in der Straßenfront als auch in der Mittelachse des Raumes durch kräftig dimensionierte, in regelmäßigen Abständen stehende Stützen unterteilt wird. Eine großflächige Leuchtdecke sorgt für eine völlig gleichmäßige Ausleuchtung des Ausstellungsareals, das durch fünf Schaufenster auf der Längsseite und weitere drei auf der Schmalseite von der Straße aus ungehindert eingesehen werden kann. Im Grunde ist der ganze Ausstellungsraum ein einziges großes Schaufenster, und dementsprechend entfaltet sich die Aktivität der Ausstellungsgestalter vor allem in der Fensterzone. Dabei handelt es sich darum, dem Laien die weitgehend abstrakte und komplizierte Entwicklung der Computertechnik und die Vorteile der IBM-Anlagen auf anschauliche Weise nahezubringen.

1–4. It was essential with this presentation of new, unfamiliar types of computers, consoles, magnetic tape storage units and other pieces of equipment that the lay public should be able to identify the individual units. Instead of the usual colour-coding or numbering a peepscope system was developed, acting on the assumption that it would arouse the curiosity of passers-by. Black plastic tubes, about 4 in in diameter, were glued to the inside of the windows, while similar tubes (which for safety were made of flexible rubber) were glued to the outside of the glass. Each of these tubes, which appeared to go right through the window, was aimed at a particular piece of equipment. Black masks cut out to follow the exact silhouette of the pieces of equipment in question were then inserted into the tubes. Finally, tongue-shaped bands of paint of various

colours were sprayed onto the windows, to draw attention to the peepscope, and, at the same time, to provide an opaque surface for the accompanying information. In the corners of the showroom itself groups of panels were hung – also tongue-shaped; one of them with an explanation of the peepscope technique.

1–4. Bei dieser Präsentation neuer, unbekannter Typen von Computern, Arbeitstischen, Magnetbandspeichern und anderem Zubehör sollte das Publikum die einzelnen Geräte genau identifizieren können. Unter Verzicht auf die übliche farbige Kennzeichnung oder Numerierung wurde ein Gucklochsystem entwickelt, von dem man zu Recht annahm, daß es die Passanten zum Durchblicken reizen würde. Auf der Innenseite der Fensterscheiben wurden schwarze

Kunststoffröhren von rund 10 cm Durchmesser geklebt, denen außen Röhren aus halbweichem schwarzem Gummi entsprachen (aus Sicherheitsgründen). Diese Röhren waren jeweils auf das Gerät gerichtet, das gezeigt werden sollte. In ihrem Inneren waren schwarze Masken eingespannt, aus denen genau die Silhouette des betreffenden Gerätes ausgeschnitten war. Um die Röhren waren zungenförmige, verschiedenfarbige Streifen auf das Fenster aufgespritzt, die als Signale auf die Gucklöcher hinwiesen. Ihre Fläche bildete zugleich eine Folie für die erläuternden Texte, die in Siebdruck auf die Scheibe aufgebracht worden waren. An den Ecken hingen im Inneren eine Gruppe von Panels, die die Zungenform der gemalten Flächen wiederholten. Eine von ihnen trug einen erklärenden Text über die Guckloch-Betrachtung.

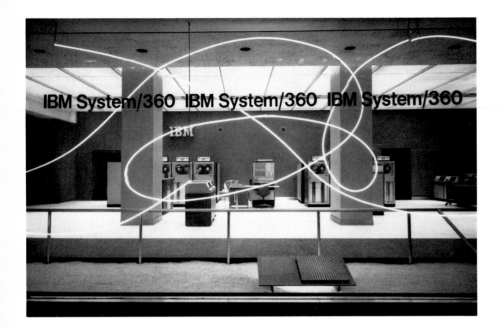

5–7. In order to demonstrate the potential of a new computer system to a public with little knowledge of the way such devices work, the designers decided to symbolize, in a way that everyone would understand, the essential characteristics of the system: speed and motion. For this purpose, they joined together sections of neon tube to form a series of loops and knots 500 ft in length. This was suspended from a waffle-patterned ceiling strip concealing the transformers and other electrical equipment required for such a construction. On the floor below a strip about 6 ft wide was covered with white marble chippings and low stands with pictures and descriptions of the new computers were placed on it.

5–7. Um die wesentlich gesteigerte Leistungsfähigkeit eines neuen Computersystems einem Laienpublikum zu demonstrieren, das kaum etwas über die Arbeitsweise solcher Geräte weiß, entschieden sich die Ausstellungsgestalter für eine allgemeinverständliche Abstraktion der Begriffe Geschwindigkeit und Bewegung. Weiße Neonröhren wurden abschnittweise zu Kurven und Schleifen zusammengesetzt. Sie wurden an einem umlaufenden, waffelartig geprägten Deckenstreifen aufgehängt, der auch die Transformatoren und sonstiges elektrisches Zubehör für die über 150 m langen Neonschlangen aufnahm. Auf dem Fußboden war ein Streifen von 1,80 m Tiefe mit weißem Marmorkies bedeckt, in dem kleine Pulte mit Abbildungen und Beschreibungen der neuen Computermodelle standen.

8–10. During the Olympic Games in Tokyo, where IBM computers were used to find out the winners within seconds, the window display of the New York showroom took the Games as its theme. Enlarged black-and-white photographs of various contests were glued onto tent-like, open-ended plastic panels of varying height, width and colour. These free-standing triangular shapes were grouped on a floor strip strewn with cork granules. Further triangles in strong primary colours added brightness to the arrangement.

8–10. Während der Olympiade in Tokio, wo IBM-Computer zu sekundenschneller Ermittlung der Sieger eingesetzt waren, nahm die Gestaltung des New Yorker Ausstellungsraums darauf Bezug. Auf zelt-förmigen, an den Seiten offenen Kunststofftafeln von verschiedener Höhe, Breite und Farbe waren vergrößerte Schwarzweißphotos verschiedener Wettkampfarten geklebt. Diese Dreiecke wurden frei-stehend auf einem mit Korkschrot bestreuten Fuß-bodenstreifen gruppiert. Weitere Dreiecke in starken Unifarben sorgten für die farbige Belebung des Ar-rangements.

77

Jewellery Shop in Mannheim

Architect: Helmut Magg, Munich
Builder: Deutsche Werkstätten, Munich

The back wall and the two side walls of this shop, which is about 30 ft × 16¹/₂ ft in area, are decorated with panels of wengé wood 3 ft 3 in wide. The display cases which are not directly attached to the walls, the partition wall and the cubical tables, used for both display and sales purposes, are all painted with matt white polyester lacquer. Above the sales tables hang silvered spotlights, while the overall lighting of the shop is provided by fluorescent tubes mounted between wooden beams running across the ceiling; the distance between these beams has been calculated so as to avoid all glare. The white ceiling itself also produces a soft reflected light. The back of the display window, near the all-glass entrance area, consists of a simple screen of boards also painted matt white with polyester lacquer.

Juweliergeschäft in Mannheim

Architekt: Helmut Magg, München
Ausführung: Deutsche Werkstätten, München

Die Rückwand und die beiden Längsseiten dieses rund 9×5 m großen Ladens sind mit etwa 1 m breiten Paneelen aus Wengéholz verkleidet. Von ihrem dunklen Holzton heben sich die frei vor der Wand befestigten Ausstellungsvitrinen ab, die ebenso wie die Trennwand und die kubischen Schau- und Verkaufstische mit mattweißem Polyesterlack gestrichen sind. Über den Verkaufstischen hängen verspiegelte Punktleuchten, während die allgemeine Raumbeleuchtung aus Leuchtstoffröhren besteht, die zwischen den quer über den Raum gespannten Brettern montiert sind. Der Abstand der Bretter ist so gewählt, daß jede Blendung vermieden wird; außerdem ergibt die hell gestrichene Decke ein weiches Reflexlicht. Die Schaufensterrückwand neben dem verglasten Eingangsbereich besteht aus einer einfachen Brettkonstruktion, die ebenfalls weiß polyesterlackiert ist.

1. View, from the entrance, of the left longitudinal wall with groups of show-cases containing large display items. A strip of white marble has been left between the beige carpet and the walls.
2. The show-cases on the right wall.
3. The entrance and the back of the display window. The gaps between the vertical boards allow the passer-by to see into the shop.
4. Floor plan.
5. One of the cubical tables with round pedestal columns.
6. Chairs behind the partition.

1. Blick vom Eingang auf die linke Längswand mit den Vitrinengruppen für größere Ausstellungsobjekte. Fußboden: beiger Spannteppich, rings umlaufender weißer Marmorfries.
2. Die frei hängenden Vitrinen der rechten Wandseite.
3. Eingang und Schaufensterrückwand. Die Abstände zwischen den vertikal montierten Brettern gestatten einen Durchblick durch das Schaufenster.
4. Grundriß.
5. Einer der kubischen Ausstellungs- und Verkaufstische auf Säulenuntergestell.
6. Sitzgruppe auf der Rückseite der Trennwand.

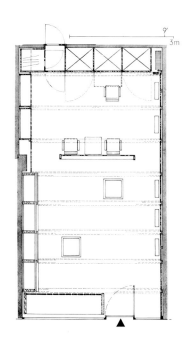

1, 2. Plan and section. Key: 1 Arcade, 2 Gallery, 3 Entrance, 4 Octagonal entrance recess, 5 Main sales room, 6 Cash-desk, 7 Staircase to basement, 8 Lift to basement, 9 Side aisle with optician's workbenches, 10 Staircase to storage gallery, 11 Sales room.
3. Overall view from the entrance.

1, 2. Grundriß und Schnitt. Legende: 1 Passage, 2 Galerie, 3 Hauseingang, 4 Oktogonale Eingangsvorhalle, 5 Großer Verkaufsraum, 6 Kasse, 7 Treppe zum Untergeschoß, 8 Fahrstuhl zum Untergeschoß, 9 »Nebenschiff« mit Werkbänken der Optik-Abteilung, 10 Treppe zur Lagergalerie, 11 Verkaufsraum.
3. Gesamtansicht vom Eingang her.

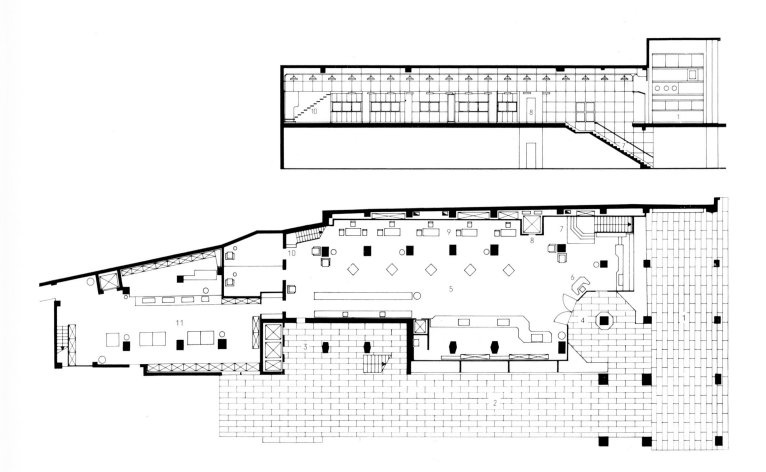

Photographic Store in Palermo

Architects: Studio Architetti BBPR (Lodovico B. Belgiojoso, Enrico Peressutti, Ernesto N. Rogers), Milan

The Randazzo photographic store, which also has an optician's department, stands on the Via Ruggero Settimo, in the centre of the city. A covered arcade in front of the store and a long side gallery leading to the lifts make the place a favourite rendezvous. Six display windows and the octagonal entrance recess attract the attention of passers-by. From this recess one can look through a glass door into the long main sales room, which was designed according to the laws of central perspective. It is divided into two aisles: the main aisle, about 12 ft 5 in high and 25 ft 6 in wide, and the side aisle, about 7 ft 10 in high and 11 ft 5 in wide, the ceiling of which was lowered to provide extra storage space above it. The olive wood panelling of the walls and the ceiling gives the whole store a sense of unity.

Photogeschäft in Palermo

Architekten: Studio Architetti BBPR (Lodovico B. Belgiojoso, Enrico Peressutti, Ernesto N. Rogers), Mailand

Das mit einer Abteilung für Augenoptik kombinierte Photogeschäft Randazzo liegt an der Straße Ruggero Settimo im Stadtzentrum. Eine vorgelagerte überdeckte Passage und eine lange seitliche Galerie, die zu einer Bucht mit Hauseingang und Fahrstühlen führt, machen es zu einem beliebten Treffpunkt. Sechs Schaufenster und eine oktogonale Eingangsnische ziehen die Aufmerksamkeit der Passanten an. Von dieser Nische aus übersieht man durch eine Glastür den langgestreckten Hauptverkaufsraum, dessen Gestaltung auf der Zentralperspektive aufbaut. Er ist in zwei »Schiffe« unterteilt: das »Hauptschiff« mit einer Höhe von 3,78 m und einer Breite von 7,80 m und das 2,38 m hohe, 3,48 m breite »Nebenschiff«, dessen Decke heruntergezogen wurde, um darüber Lagerraum zu gewinnen. Die Wand- und Deckenverkleidung mit genormten Platten aus Olivenholz bildet ein warmgetöntes einheitliches Gehäuse.

4. View from the interior of the store looking towards the entrance recess with the octagonal show-case around the supporting pillar. On the left, near the glass door of the entrance, the cash-desk. Further to the left, the lower side aisle with the staircase to the basement. Floor of concrete topped with marble mosaic (Designer: Roberto Sambonet).
5. Oblique view of the main room and the adjacent optician's department.

4. Blick vom Ladeninneren gegen das Oktogon der Eingangsvorhalle mit der Achteck-Vitrine um den Stützpfeiler. Links von der Glastür des Eingangs die Kasse. Ganz links das niedrigere »Nebenschiff« mit der Treppe zum Untergeschoß. Fußboden aus Zementplatten mit Marmor-Mosaik (Entwurf: Roberto Sambonet).
5. Schrägansicht von Hauptraum und anschließender, niedrigerer Optik-Abteilung.

6. One of the two display windows facing the arcade. Its back wall is also panelled with olive wood. Two sections on the right are left open to show the interior with the stairs to the basement.

7. One of the five show-cases with brass frames and pedestals which run the length of the main room. Behind it a table which is used as both a counter and a work-bench by the optician's department.

8. Detail of the staircase to the storage gallery over the side aisle. The olive wood panels on the long walls can be easily removed so that show-cases or shelves can be fitted instead. Lighting: flat cushion-shaped bowls with brass fittings suspended from the ceiling in the main aisle and fitted directly to the ceiling elsewhere.

6. Eines der beiden Schaufenster an der Passage. Seine Rückwand ist ebenfalls mit Olivenholzplatten verkleidet. Zwei Felder der rechten Hälfte sind offen und geben den Blick in das Innere, auf die Treppe zum Untergeschoß, frei.

7. Eine der fünf in Längsrichtung aufgestellten Vitrinen mit Rahmen und Sockel aus dunklem Messing. Dahinter ein Verkaufs- und Werktisch der Optik-Abteilung.

8. Detail mit Treppenaufgang zur Lagergalerie über dem »Nebenschiff«. Die aufgeschraubten Olivenholzplatten der Wand- und Deckenverkleidung sind links besonders gut zu erkennen. An den Längswänden können die Wandplatten abgenommen und statt dessen Vitrinen oder Schubkastenelemente eingesetzt werden. Beleuchtung durch flache Deckenschalen mit Messinghalterungen, im »Hauptschiff« frei unter der Decke hängend.

AgfaFoto Branch Store in Catania, Italy

Architect: Giancarlo Pozzo, Milan

The showroom and the customers' waiting-room, which are combined with an office, are located on the ground floor of a new building of which the Agfa branch store occupies two storeys. To make one large unified space, all unnecessary partition walls were removed. Since the existing pillars and the ceiling girders varied in size, a way had to be found to make the room both aesthetically and functionally effective. This was done by facing the pillars in brick and extending the sides to form recesses. These recesses contain light-boxes for displaying transparencies, and shelves for other goods. Materials: marble floors; white walls and ceilings; recesses dark brown on the inside with edges of dark grey, lacquered metal; doors, counters and other woodwork in walnut.

Filiale der Firma AgfaFoto in Catania, Italien

Architekt: Giancarlo Pozzo, Mailand

Der Ausstellungs- und Kundenwarteraum, kombiniert mit einem Büroraum für Publikumsverkehr, liegt im Hochparterre eines Neubaus, in dem die Agfa-Filiale zwei Stockwerke bezogen hat. Um einen großzügigen, zusammenhängenden Raum zu erhalten, wurden alle überflüssigen Zwischenwände herausgenommen. Da die Stützen und Deckenbalken der Tragkonstruktion unterschiedlich dimensioniert und unregelmäßig verteilt waren, mußte versucht werden, dem Raum eine ästhetisch und funktional befriedigende Ordnung zu geben. Das wurde erreicht, indem man die Stützen mit Mauerwerscheiben ummantelte, die jeweils nach zwei Seiten offene Nischen bilden. In die Nischen sind Leuchtkästen mit Diapositiven und Fachborde als Warenträger eingebaut. Materialien: Marmorfußboden; Wände und Decken weiß; Nischeninneres braun, Einfassung der Nischen aus dunkelgrau lackierten Metallprofilen; Türen, Theke und sonstige Holzteile Nußbaum.

1. View from the customers' waiting-room looking towards the counter, the lower parts of which serve as display cases. In the background, the office area. Customers' room: blue woollen carpet; seats from a standard Arflex range. Office: chairs, filing cabinets and desks (MMG series) by Herman Miller. The desks have orange bases and white plastic tops. Lighting fixtures by Studio Artemide.
2. Detail of recess. Glass-topped display tables with metal (T-section) frames.
3. Floor plan. Key: 1 Entrance, 2 Display in the ante-room, 3 Customers' waiting-room with seating, 4 Counter with display cases, 5 Display tables, 6 Recess with light-boxes, 7 Office, 8 Interior stairway to basement.
4. View from the customers' room of the display tables in the ante-room near the entrance. On the end wall are enlargements of photographs.

1. Blick vom Kundenwarteraum über die Theke, deren Unterteile rechts und links als Ausstellungsvitrinen dienen, auf den Büroteil im Hintergrund. Kundenraum: blauer Wollteppich; serienmäßige Sessel der Firma ArFlex. Büro: Stühle, Registraturschränke und Schreibtische (Serie MMG) von Herman Miller mit orangefarben lackierten Korpussen und weißen Schichtstoffplatten. Lampen: Studio Artemide.
2. Detailansicht einer Nische. Ausstellungstische mit Glasplatte auf T-Metallprofilen.
3. Grundriß. Legende: 1 Eingang, 2 Ausstellung im Vorraum, 3 Kundenwarteraum mit Sitzgruppe, 4 Theke mit Ausstellungsvitrinen, 5 Ausstellungstische, 6 Nische mit Leuchtkasten, 7 Büro, 8 interne Treppe zum Untergeschoß.
4. Blick vom Kundenraum auf die Ausstellungstische im Vorraum beim Eingang. An der Rückwand Großphotos.

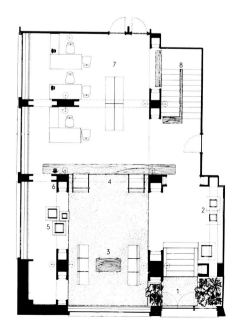

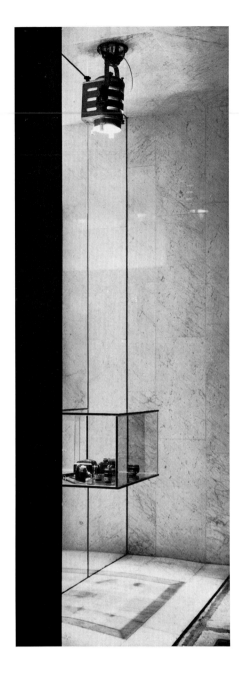

Camera shop in Oslo

Architect: Sverre Fehn, Oslo
Technical consultant: Arne Neegård

Photogeschäft in Oslo

Architekt: Sverre Fehn, Oslo
Technische Beratung: Arne Neegård

The ground floor of an old building in Prinsens Gate, in the centre of Oslo, was converted into this branch store of Fotohuset. To make the room appear larger, the counter, a block 13 ft 9 in long, 3 ft wide and 1 ft 5 in high, was designed completely in glass. One end of it extends 1 ft 9 in through the toughened laminated glass shop front to act as a show-case, giving passers-by the opportunity of a close inspection of the cameras on display. The side walls and the floor are faced with marble, and the end wall displays a greatly enlarged photograph of frost on grass. All storage units, as well as the low work table and the stools, are made of Oregon pine, and were designed by the architect. Large spotlights on pivots provide the lighting for the counter and the end wall.

Für dieses Zweiggeschäft der Firma Fotohuset wurde das Erdgeschoß eines alten Gebäudes in der Prinsens Gate, mitten im Zentrum von Oslo, umgebaut. Um den Raum größer erscheinen zu lassen, ist der Ladentisch als Ganzglaskonstruktion in Form eines liegenden Blocks von 4,19 m Länge, 0,85 m Breite und 0,43 m Höhe ausgebildet. Er durchstößt die Glasfront des Ladens und ragt als Ausstellungsvitrine 0,53 m über die Fassade aus vergütetem Schichtglas hinaus. Passanten können so die ausgestellten Photoapparate aus nächster Nähe betrachten. Die Längswände und der Fußboden sind mit Marmorplatten verkleidet, während die Rückwand eine riesige Photovergrößerung »Gräser im Rauhreif« trägt. Sämtliche Schränke, der niedrige Arbeitstisch und die Hocker wurden nach Entwürfen des Architekten in Oregon Pine ausgeführt. Für die Beleuchtung sind große, schwenkbare Scheinwerfer eingesetzt, die den Ladentisch und die Rückwand anstrahlen.

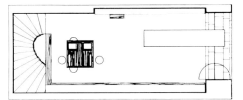

1, 2. Oblique and front view of the display case which extends through the glass facade. A spotlight fixed to the ceiling on the street side of the shop front projects an interesting silhouette of the display onto the floor.

3, 4. Longitudinal section and plan of the shop.

5. Overall view from Prinsens Gate. Heating elements are installed in the ceiling outside the shop as well as inside, in order to prevent stresses within the glass.

1, 2. Schräg- und Frontalansicht der vorspringenden Vitrine in der Ganzglasfassade. Ein Deckenscheinwerfer vor der Glasfront wirft ein Schattenmuster des Schaukastens auf den Boden.

3, 4. Längsschnitt und Grundriß des Ladens.

5. Gesamtansicht von der Prinsens Gate aus. Die Heizschlangen der Deckenstrahlungsheizung sind auch vor die Fassade gezogen, um Spannungen im Glas zu vermeiden.

6, 7. The care with which the store was designed is apparent in the details. On the left, as an example of the furniture designed by the architect, is a stool of Oregon pine; the seat is covered with natural oxhide. On the right. a side view of the protruding display case as seen from the all-glass entrance door.
8. View from the basement, of the winding staircase leading up to the shop, and arriving in front of the end wall. The banisters are upright strips of toughened glass. The architect has used glass and sensitized paper extensively to establish a close relationship between his design and the photographic lenses and modern precision cameras on display.

6, 7. Für die Sorgfalt, mit der dieser Laden gestaltet wurde, sprechen auch die Details. Links ein Beispiel der vom Architekten entworfenen Möblierung: ein Hocker aus Oregon Pine, Sitzfläche mit naturfarbenem Rindsleder bezogen. Rechts die Seitenansicht der vorspringenden Ausstellungsvitrine, von der Nurglastür des Eingangs aus gesehen.
8. Blick vom Untergeschoß auf die geschwungene Treppe, die vor der Rückwand mit dem Großphoto in den Laden hinaufführt. Senkrecht stehende Streifen aus vergütetem Glas bilden das Treppengeländer. Die Verwendung von Glas und lichtempfindlichem Papier ist nicht zufällig. Der Architekt wollte bewußt eine Beziehung zur photographischen Linse und zur Präzision eines Photoapparates herstellen.

9, 10. The laminated glass banister plates, 4 ft 2 in high and 10 in wide, are carried by 3/8 in stainless steel bolts, with hexagonal nuts and steel washers. The annular plastic shims prevent the glass from cracking and make the fastening flexible.

9, 10. Die 128 cm hohen und 25 cm breiten Schichtglasscheiben des Treppengeländers werden von 10 mm starken Bolzen aus rostfreiem Stahl gehalten und mit Sechskantmuttern zwischen Distanzringen aus Stahl verschraubt. Zwischenringe aus Kunststoff verhindern ein Springen des Glases und ermöglichen seine elastische Befestigung.

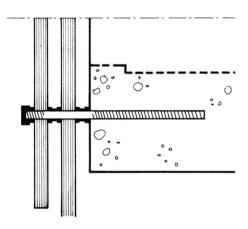

Camera Shop in Milan

Architect: Joe Colombo, Milan

Photogeschäft in Mailand

Architekt: Joe Colombo, Mailand

In the design of this camera shop the architect used the shape of the optical lens as a leitmotif. The display cases consist of Plexiglas domes fitted to provide either a convex or a concave surface. The dome shape is repeated in the hundreds of small hemispheres set in the ceiling, which is itself covered with chromium-plated sheet polythene of the kind used in Christmas decorations. The hemispheres act as mirrors, thereby increasing the perspective of the ceiling. This perspective distortion is still further heightened by the stepped back wall. A trap into which many photographic shops fall – having too many articles on show – was avoided by placing the display items under the Plexiglas domes. This leaves 80% of the room free, and gives the customer the chance to inspect the equipment at close range.

Beim Entwurf dieses Ladens für Photo- und Filmbedarf stand als Leitmotiv die Form der optischen Linse Pate: Die Ausstellungsvitrinen bestehen aus konvexen und konkaven Plexiglaskuppeln, die ihr Gegenstück in den Hunderten kleiner, halbkugelförmiger Wölbungen der Decke finden. Diese ist mit verchromten Folien aus Kunststoff verkleidet, wie sie für Christbaumschmuck verwendet werden. Die darin eingeprägten Halbkugeln brechen als Spiegel das Licht und steigern die perspektivische Wirkung der Decke – ein Effekt, der im Verkaufsraum noch durch die stufenweise Abtreppung der Rückwand unterstrichen wird. Die Gefahr einer basarähnlichen Überfüllung ist hier durch die Ordnung und Zusammenfassung der Ausstellungsobjekte unter den Plexiglashauben vermieden. So können 80% des Raumes freigelassen und die Apparate in Nahsicht betrachtet werden.

1. Night view of the sales room looking over the free-standing, dome-shaped show-case towards the entrance and the display window, the plate glass of which reflects the stepped rear wall and the hemispheres of the ceiling.
2. Plan of sales room (A), projection-room (B), and workshop with stock rooms (C). For key see above right.
3. Overall view from the street. On the left the sales room with the convex wall-cases and display tables. On the right, the circular window in front of the projection-room; behind it, a shelf-unit of planks cut to form a concave variant of the lens shape.

1. Blick bei Nacht durch den Verkaufsraum über die frei stehende Kuppelvitrine hinweg auf Eingang und Schaufenster, in deren Scheiben sich die abgetreppte Rückwand und die Kugeldecke spiegeln.
2. Grundriß von Verkaufsraum (A), Vorführraum für Projektionsapparate (B) und Werkstatt mit Lager (C). Legende siehe oben rechts.
3. Gesamtansicht von der Straße aus. Links der Verkaufsraum mit den konvexen Wand- und Tischvitrinen. Rechts der kreisförmige Schaufensterausschnitt vor dem Vorführraum; dahinter bildet ein Regal mit entsprechend zurechtgesägten Brettern eine große konkave Vitrine, die die Linsenform einmal mehr variiert.

Key: 1 Entrance, 2 Free-standing display case with convex Plexiglas dome, 3 Wall show-cases, 4 Counter and light-box, 5 Cylindrical cases for films, 6 Entrance to workshop and stockroom can be closed off by strip-rubber screen, 7 Work-benches, 8 Rear entrance, 9 Passage to the projection-room; also with strip-rubber screen, 10 Concave display case, 11 Blind of rubber strips, 12 Projection-table, 13 Projection-screen.

Legende zum Grundriß: 1 Eingang, 2 Frei stehende Vitrine mit konvexer Plexiglaskuppel, 3 Wandvitrinen, 4 Laden- und Leuchttisch, 5 Röhrenregale für Filme, 6 Mit Gummistreifen verdeckbarer Durchgang zu Werkstatt und Lager, 7 Arbeitstische, 8 Hintereingang, 9 Mit Gummistreifen verdeckbarer Durchgang zum Vorführraum für Projektionsapparate, 10 Konkave Schaufenstervitrine, 11 Verdunkelungsvorhang aus Gummistreifen, 12 Projektionstisch, 13 Projektionsleinwand.

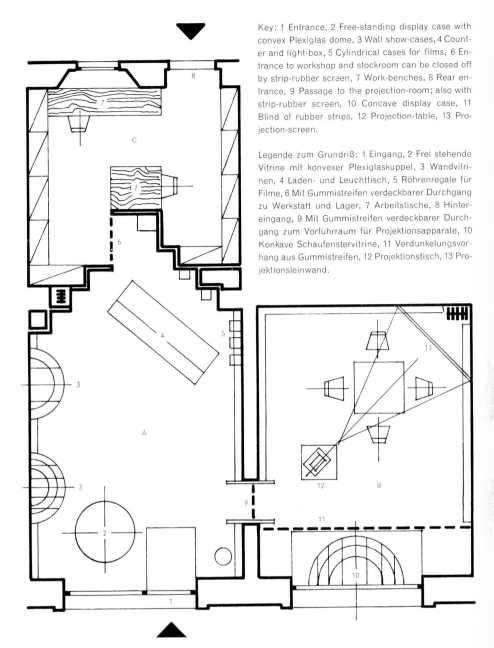

4. The change in the height of the ceiling divides the sales room into a higher front half and a lower back half. The black rubber floor-covering rounds off the angle at the foot of the wall and is continued up to about knee-height. The brick bases of the free-standing show-case and counter are similarly treated.
5. An eye-catching, semi-silhouette effect is achieved by placing the items on display in the convex cases in front of squares of white translucent Plexiglas lit from behind.

4. Ein Sprung in der Deckenhöhe teilt den Verkaufsraum in eine höhere vordere Hälfte (rechts) und in eine niedrigere hintere. Die Deckenverkleidung aus verchromten Halbkugeln folgt dieser Höhenversetzung. Der Fußbodenbelag aus schwarzem Gummi ist an den Wänden halbkreisförmig ausgekehlt und bis über Kniehöhe als Sockel weitergeführt. Auch die gemauerten Unterteile der freistehenden Vitrine und des Ladentisches wurden in der gleichen Weise verkleidet.
5. Quadratische Flächen im Inneren der konvexen Wandvitrinen sind mit durchscheinendem weißen Plexiglas verkleidet und von rückwärts beleuchtbar. Dadurch werden die Silhouetten der Ausstellungsobjekte effektvoll betont.

6. The rear part of the sales room with the stepped back wall and the obliquely placed counter, which doubles as a display table. There is also a built-in light-box for the inspection of negatives. To protect delicate equipment, part of the counter is covered with a strip of rubber. Cylindrical cases, for films and other small objects, are fixed to the walls.

6. Der hintere Teil des Verkaufsraums mit der abgetreppten Rückwand und der schräggestellten Verkaufstheke, die auch als Leuchttisch mit eingebautem Lichtkasten zur Betrachtung von Negativen dient. Zum Schutz der empfindlichen Apparate ist ein weiterer Teil der Tischplatte mit einem Gummistreifen abgedeckt. An den Wänden zylinderförmige Kästen für Filme und Kleinmaterial.

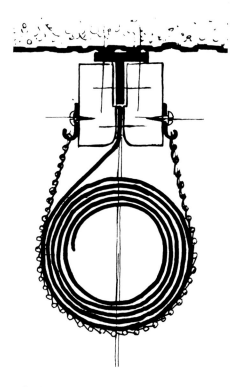

7. Blinds made of black rubber strips are used to darken the room. They can be pulled up and fastened with a small chain.

8. View from the projection-room into the sales room.

9. The wooden framework of the concave display case seen from behind.

10, 11. The lighting fixtures, like the rest of the fittings, were designed by the architect. They provide a variation on the lens theme.

7, 8. Durchblick aus dem Vorführraum für Projektionsapparate in den Verkaufsraum. Zur Verdunkelung dienen Vorhänge aus schwarzen Gummistreifen, die nach oben gerollt und mit einem Kettchen festgehalten werden können.

9. Das Holzgestell der konkaven Schaufenstervitrine von innen gesehen.

10, 11. Auch die Lampen wurden, wie die gesamte Einrichtung, vom Architekten entworfen. Sie variieren ebenfalls die Linsenform.

Candleshop in Vienna

Architect: Hans Hollein, Vienna

The Retti Candleshop in which the products of the Innsbruck wax goods factory of Messrs. Marius Retti are sold, is located in the Kohlmarkt and has a floor area of only 160 square feet and a frontage of barely 13 feet. It is part of a building of about 1900. The new shop is a distinguished and elegant solution of great technical perfection and in sharp contrast with the eclectic architecture of the older building. The flow of space from the outside continues into the interior with no change of materials, brushed and anodized aluminium being generally used throughout the shop either glued with epoxy resin or partially screwed. The interior is characterized by a clear functionalism and a maximum economy of space. It has a certain spaciousness in spite of its most limited size which was mainly achieved by the sequence of narrowing and opening spaces.

Kerzenfachgeschäft in Wien

Architekt: Hans Hollein, Wien

Der Retti-Kerzenladen am Kohlmarkt, in dem die Produkte des Innsbrucker Wachswarenwerkes Marius Retti verkauft werden, hat eine Bodenfläche von nur 14,8 m² und eine Frontlänge von knapp 4 m. Er wurde in ein um 1900 entstandenes Gebäude eingebaut, dessen eklektischer Architektur eine technisch perfekte, exklusive und elegante Lösung gegenübergestellt ist. Außen und Innen gehen ineinander über, auch im Material gibt es keine Trennung: Durchweg ist vorzugsweise geschliffenes und eloxiertes Aluminium verwendet, das mit Epoxyd-Harz geklebt oder zum Teil auch verschraubt wurde. Beim Ladeninnern, das sich durch klare Funktionalität und maximale Raumausnutzung auszeichnet, konnte trotz größter Enge eine gewisse Weitläufigkeit erzielt werden, was hauptsächlich durch die Abfolge sich verengender und erweiternder Raumteile erreicht ist.

1. View into the square exhibition room which is set diagonally to the street. The technical installations, such as the air conditioning equipment over the entrance door, are integral parts of the spatial concept. Floor-to-ceiling mirrors are set on the diagonal axis; rust-red, fitted moquette carpet, the walls of the niches are covered in cognac-coloured shantung.
2. Perspective drawing of the sequence of rooms which were designed to balance symmetrically about an axis. The narrow entranceway and the closed front arouse curiosity; the interior expands towards the exhibition area, opens for a moment into the indefinite, due to the two facing mirrors, and narrows again to form a second passageway leading into the storage and sales area. All this provides a dynamic development of space in a very small area.
3, 4. Day and night view of the almost totally closed street front. Through the upper section of the porch which is strongly accented, the interior lighting is visible. At both sides of the door soffit, the name of the firm in plastic lettering. The showcases are set at an angle of 45° to the passers-by.

1. Blick in den übereck gedrehten Ausstellungsraum. Die technischen Einrichtungen wie das Klimagerät über der Eingangstür sind völlig integriert. In der Querachse raumhohe Spiegel. Rostroter Velour-Teppichboden, Wandbespannung der Nischen kognakfarbener Shantung.
2. Perspektive der axial und symmetrisch angelegten Raumfolge. Die Enge des Eingangs und die Geschlossenheit der Front weckt Neugierde. Der Innenraum weitet sich in den Ausstellungsbereich, dehnt sich mit Hilfe der beiden gegenüberliegenden Spiegel für einen Moment ins Unendliche aus, um sich zu einer zweiten Passage zu verengen, die in das Verkaufslager führt: Dynamisierung des Raumerlebnisses.
3, 4. Tag- und Nachtansicht der nahezu geschlossenen Straßenfront. Im expressiv betonten oberen Portalausschnitt Innenbeleuchtung sichtbar. In der Türlaibung beidseits Firmennamen aus plastischen Buchstaben. Vitrinen um 45° den Passanten zugewandt.

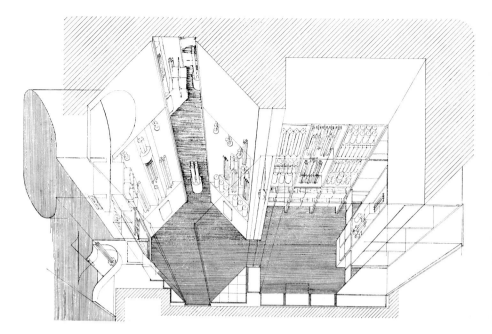

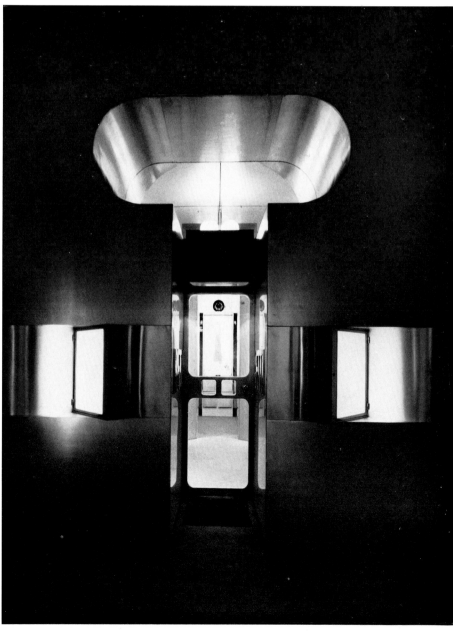

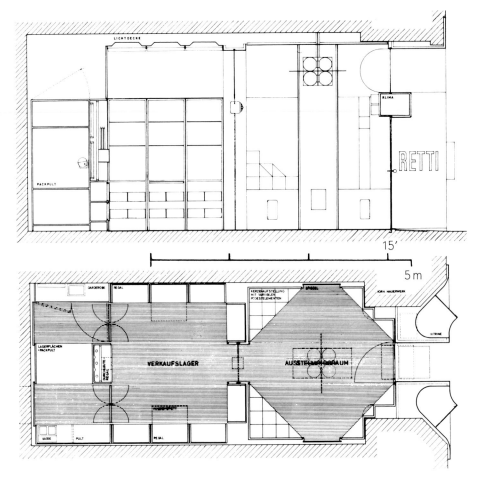

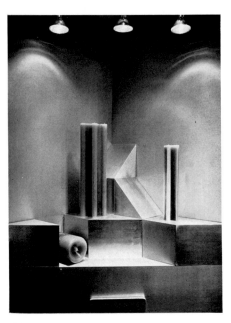

5. Lighting fittings made of glass spheres and chrome plated steel are suspended at the intersection of the main axes in the exhibition area.

6, 7. Longitudinal section and plan.

8. Street front with one of the two aluminium lined showcases which are set at 45° to the facade and towards the passers-by.

9. A system of display holders (cubes and prisms of aluminium) make it possible to display the candles in a great number of different ways.

10. View towards the entrance showing the oval opening over the door.

11. Floor-to-ceiling mirrors set in the angles of the cross axis make the display area appear larger than it actually is.

12. Diagram of the spatial concept.

13. View from the storage area where the customers are served. A counter was dispensed with in order to avoid a separating barrier. Display shelves have light grey plastic facing.

14. The cash register and the packing table are separated from the storage and sales area open to the public by small aluminium swinging doors. Central illuminated showcase for the exhibition of translucent candles; the interesting interior structure of these becomes visible in a similar way when they burn down.

5. Beleuchtungskörper aus Glaskugeln und verchromtem Stahlblech im Schnittpunkt der Hauptachsen im Ausstellungsraum.

6, 7. Längsschnitt und Grundriß.

8. Straßenfront mit einer der beiden aluminiumverkleideten Vitrinen, die um 45° den Passanten entgegengedreht sind.

9. In den Nischen des Ausstellungsraums erlauben variable Podestelemente (Würfel und Prismen aus Aluminium) eine Vielzahl von Aufstellungsmöglichkeiten der Kerzen.

10. Blick zum Eingang mit dem Oval der oberen Portalöffnung.

11. In der Querachse schaffen raumhohe Spiegel eine optische Erweiterung des Ausstellungsraums, die ihn sehr viel größer wirken läßt.

12. Diagramm der Raumkonzeption.

13. Durchblick vom Verkaufslager, wo die Kunden bedient werden. Verzicht auf Verkaufspult, um die trennende Barriere zu vermeiden. Regale mit hellgrauer Kunststoffbeschichtung.

14. Die Bereiche der Kasse und des Packtisches sind vom öffentlich zugänglichen Verkaufslager durch Aluminium-Schwingtürchen abgegrenzt. Mittelvitrine zum Durchleuchten von Kerzen mit interessanter Innenstruktur, die auch beim Abbrennen sichtbar wird.

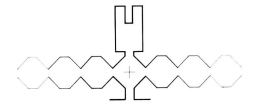

Interior Decoration Shop in Basle

Architects: Max Rasser and Tibère Vadi, Basle

In a new building in the old part of the city, with a site of only 120 square yards at their disposal, Messrs. Domus had to arrange the various departments over four floors. In the basement, ceramics and basket ware are sold. Floor-to-ceiling show windows allow a clear view into the ground floor where a variety of sales displays are arranged. On the first floor, glasses, china and hardware are sold; on the second floor furniture, textiles and wall-papers. The upper floors are likewise glazed to full height, partially with clear glass, partially with translucent. Circular light fittings mounted flush with the ceiling produce a uniform general illumination which is accentuated by spotlights. The two upper floors have wall-to-wall carpets; the floor finish of the ground floor is ground and polished marble pebbles set in a cement matrix.

Einrichtungshaus in Basel

Architekten: Max Rasser und Tibère Vadi, Basel

Bei nur 100 m² Grundfläche, die der Firma Domus in einem Neubau in der engen Altstadt zur Verfügung standen, sind die verschiedenen Abteilungen über vier Geschosse verteilt. Im Untergeschoß werden Keramik und Korbwaren verkauft, im Erdgeschoß, das durch raumhohe Schaufenster zu übersehen ist, finden wechselnde Verkaufsausstellungen statt, im ersten Obergeschoß werden Glaswaren, Geschirr und Bestecke angeboten, im zweiten Obergeschoß Möbel, Stoffe und Tapeten. Die oberen Stockwerke sind ebenfalls in voller Höhe verglast, teils mit Klarglas, teils mit durchscheinendem Strukturglas. Bündig in die Decke eingelassene Leuchten ergeben eine gleichmäßige Allgemeinbeleuchtung, die durch Punktstrahler akzentuiert ist. Die beiden Obergeschosse wurden mit Spannteppichen ausgelegt, der Fußboden des Erdgeschosses besteht aus geschliffenen Marmorkieseln.

1. Total view of the new corner building. The sales room on the ground floor can be looked into from the street on two sides.
2. The sales room on the ground floor reserved for a variety of displays with set-back display window facade which has no glazing bars.
3. Display of Swedish ceramics on the ground floor. Blacksprayed L-shaped iron units with standardized dimensions are used as tables or are mounted to form stands of various heights. The partitions between the shelves are of jute.
4. On the first floor, the silhouettes and colours of the objects on display in front of the translucent walls of structural glass, show off effectively. Stands made of L-shaped iron elements with shelves of glass, white or black Marbrit.
5, 6. Plan of an upper floor and of the ground floor (below).
7. Wood wall with adjustable glass shelves resting on iron brackets set in pre-drilled holes.

1. Gesamtansicht des Eckhaus-Neubaus. Der Verkaufsraum im Erdgeschoß ist von zwei Straßenseiten aus einzusehen.
2. Der Wechselausstellungen vorbehaltene Verkaufsraum im Erdgeschoß mit sprossenlos verglaster, zurückgesetzter Schaufensterfront.
3. Ausstellung schwedischer Keramik im Erdgeschoß. Schwarz gespritzte Winkeleisen-Elemente mit genormten Maßen werden als Tische verwendet oder zu Gestellen von unterschiedlicher Höhe aufgebaut. Trennstreifen zwischen den Vitrinen aus Jute.
4. Vor den durchscheinenden Strukturglaswänden im ersten Obergeschoß werden Silhouetten und Farben der Ausstellungsobjekte besonders betont. Winkeleisengestelle mit Fachborden aus Rohglas, weißem oder schwarzem Marbrit.
5, 6. Grundriß eines Obergeschosses und des Erdgeschosses (unten).
7. Holzwand mit verstellbaren Glastablaren, die auf Rundeisenbolzen in vorgebohrten Löchern aufgelegt werden.

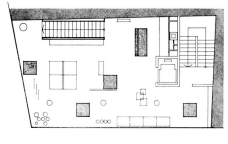

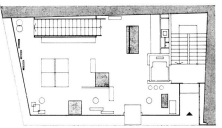

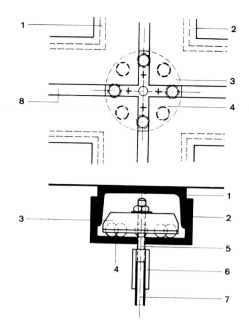

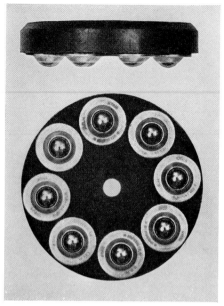

Rosenthal Studio Building in Düsseldorf

Design: Rosenthal Studio B, Selb
(Team of Ingeborg August, Hans Peter Piel,
Claus Cullmann)
Co-planning and management of building operations: E. and G. Kuhn, Düsseldorf

Rosenthal AG converted a former dance hall on Königsallee in Düsseldorf into a store to sell glassware and porcelain goods designed by artists with international reputations. With a relatively narrow street front, about 46 ft wide, an adaptable window display system was developed which could present as many articles as possible to the great number of passers-by on this main business street. Tracks built into the suspended ceiling carry Plexiglas and wood panels on a module of about 28 × 28 in as well as the doors and walls of showcases, which can all be shifted and turned as required. The rollers, on which the partitions are suspended, guarantee an easy passage at the track crossings. Considerable changes of the store ground plan can be effected overnight; and as much as 250 ft of show window front erected.

Rosenthal-Studiohaus in Düsseldorf

Entwurf: Rosenthal Studio B, Selb
(Team Ingeborg August, Hans Peter Piel,
Claus Cullmann)
Mitplanung und Bauleitung: E. und G. Kuhn,
Düsseldorf

Für den Verkauf von Glas- und Porzellanwaren international bekannter Designer ließ die Rosenthal AG. in Düsseldorf ein ehemaliges Tanzcafé an der Königsallee umbauen. Um dem starken Passantenstrom dieser Hauptgeschäftsstraße trotz der verhältnismäßig schmalen Frontbreite von nur 14 m ein möglichst umfassendes Warenangebot vorführen zu können, wurde eine variable Schaufensteranlage entwickelt: In Laufschienen, die mit einem Modul von 70 × 70 cm in die untergehängte Decke eingebaut sind, können Wandelemente aus Sicherheitsglas oder Holztafeln, aber auch Türen und Vitrinenwände beliebig verschoben und gedreht werden. Die Rollenköpfe, an denen die Scheiben aufgehängt sind, überwinden mühelos die Schienenkreuzungen. Selbst extreme Veränderungen des Ladengrundrisses sind in einer Nacht möglich; maximal lassen sich 77 m Schaufensterfront gewinnen.

1. View of the ceiling, and section through the suspension system of the moveable display window panes and wood partitions (after patent drawing). Key: 1 U-profile section, 2 Angle iron serving as guide rail, 3 Roller, 4 Set-in ball, 5 Connecting bolt at ball guiding assembly, 6 Fastening of pane, 7 Pane or partition, 8 Slot for connecting bolt in guide channel.
2. View of roller as seen from the side and from below.
3. Display windows and show-cases arranged after variant C of the floor plan, as seen from Königsallee.
4, 5. Longitudinal section and ground floor plan.
6–9. Variants of floor plan showing various possibilities of layout for the flexible sales-areas. The darker fields mark show-cases, display windows and sales-areas; the white fields represent the sales-areas open to the street. Variant A: Interior display cases arranged step-wise. Variant B: Sharply recessed sales-area; at the front part of the store, six show-cases arranged at right angles with the street front. Variant C (see fig. 3): Three square show-cases on the street front, with a long show-case placed behind them. Variant D: The island of the front part of the store is surrounded by a circulation area.

1. Deckenansicht und Schnitt durch die Aufhängevorrichtung der beweglichen Schaufensterscheiben und Holzwände (nach der Patentzeichnung). Legende: 1 U-Profil, 2 Winkel als Gleitschiene, 3 Rollenkopf, 4 eingelassene Kugel, 5 Verbindungsbolzen am Kugellaufwerk, 6 Befestigung der Scheibe, 7 Scheibe oder Trennwand, 8 Nute für Verbindungsbolzen in der Gleitschiene.
2. Ansicht des Rollenkopfes von der Seite und von unten.
3. Schaufenster und Vitrinen in der Anordnung nach Grundrißvariante C, von der Königsallee aus gesehen.
4, 5. Längsschnitt und Grundriß des Erdgeschosses.
6–9. Grundrißvarianten mit verschiedenen Möglichkeiten für die Aufteilung der Nutzfläche. Die getönten Flächen markieren Vitrinen, Schaufenster und Ladenfläche; die weißen Flächen kennzeichnen von der Straße aus zugängliche Verkaufsflächen. Variante A: Abgetreppte Innenschaufenster. Variante B: Weit zurückgezogener Verkaufsraum, im vorderen Ladenteil sechs Vitrinen rechtwinklig zur Straßenfront. Variante C (siehe Abb. 3): Drei quadratische Vitrinen an der Straße, dahinter ein langer quergestellter Schaukasten. Variante D: Ein Umgang umschließt den inselförmigen vorderen Ladenteil.

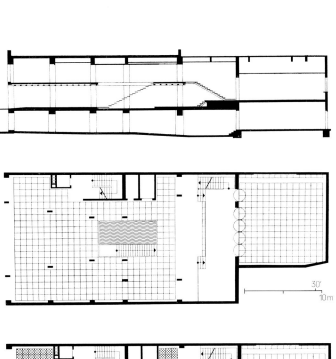

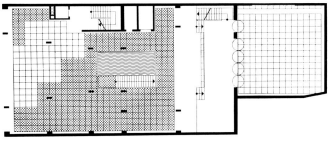

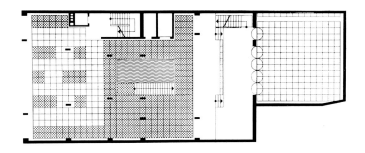

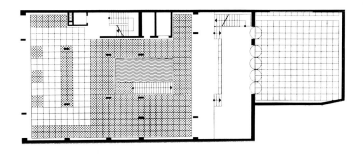

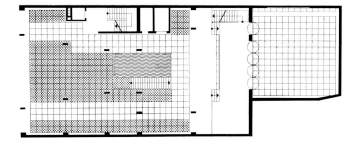

10. View of the ground floor with the water pool and the transparent Plexiglas staircase, beyond are the street-front and show-cases. At the suspended ceiling, the sections of the grid with guide channels. Lighting by 668 ceiling reflectors, each of them is controlled by an independent switch.

11. Detail view of the show-cases made up of glass and wood panels in a variety of combinations.

12. The all-Plexiglas staircase, about 16 ft long, leading to the sales room on the first floor.

10. Blick durch das Erdgeschoß mit Wasserbecken und transparenter Plexiglastreppe auf die Vitrinen an der Straße. In der untergehängten Decke die Rasterfelder mit den Gleitschienen. Beleuchtung durch insgesamt 668 einzeln schaltbare Deckenstrahler.

11. Detailansicht der variablen Vitrinenkombination aus beweglichen Glas- und Holzwänden.

12. Die 5 m lange, völlig aus Plexiglas hergestellte Treppe zum Verkaufsraum im 1. Obergeschoß.

13. The interior, including wall shelves, show-cases and tables was designed on a specific modular system. Special lighting effects can be produced by luminous boxes radiating upwards and downwards, which can be suspended between the square section steel shelf supports. All wooden parts, including the wall panelling, are either of Sen ashwood or Wengé. Basalt lava tiles were used as floor covering in the adjustable sales-areas, all other rooms have fitted carpets.

14. Wall brackets with adjustable glass shelves, free-standing shelves with suspended luminous boxes and the islands of the display tables, all made of standardized elements, guarantee a great number of display variations.

15. Room for special exhibitions with a display of objects by Tapio Wirkkala. Floor-to-ceiling Plexiglas panes can be suspended from the wood frame of the ceiling grid. Along with the wood or glass display shelves, they produce a display system of great transparency.

13. Die Innenausstattung mit Regalen, Vitrinen und Tischen folgt ebenfalls einem einheitlichen Maßsystem. Besondere Effekte lassen sich durch die nach oben und unten strahlenden Leuchtkästen erzielen, die zwischen die Vierkantstahlrohre der Regale eingehängt werden können. Alle Holzteile, auch die Wandverkleidungen, bestehen entweder aus Senesche oder aus Wengé. Für den Fußboden des variablen Verkaufsteils sind Basaltlavaplatten verwendet, alle anderen Räume sind mit Spannteppichen ausgelegt.

14. Wandregale mit verstellbaren Glastablaren, frei stehende Regale mit eingehängten Leuchtkästen und die inselförmigen Ausstellungstische aus genormten Elementen ermöglichen eine äußerst flexible Ausstellungsgestaltung.

15. Der Raum für Sonderausstellungen mit einer Schau der Arbeiten von Tapio Wirkkala. Am Holzgitter des Deckenrasters können raumhohe Platten aus Sicherheitsglas befestigt werden, die zusammen mit Holz- oder Glastablaren ein in hohem Maße transparentes Regalsystem bilden.

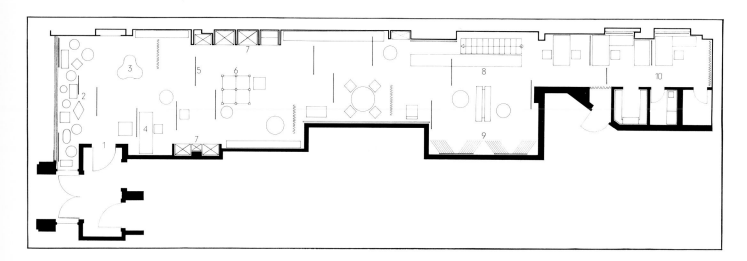

Display Room 'Textiles & Objects' of Herman Miller Inc. in New York

Architect: Alexander Girard, Santa Fé, New Mexico

In the fabric shop of the Herman Miller Collection in Manhattan, 8 East 53rd Street, which was designed by Alexander Girard, the architect-designer combined a merchandising display of fabrics for curtains and upholstery with a fascinating selection of popular art and craft objects from various parts of the world. The rich variety of forms and the brilliant colours of these objects combine with the textiles to create a fantastic and amusing atmosphere. Instead of displaying the fabrics by decorating windows as simulated room settings, the textiles were treated in the same way as the objects of popular art from Mexico and Peru, i.e. as the decorative elements of an exhibition which was designed to appeal to the public's imagination.

Ausstellungsraum »Textiles & Objects« der Herman Miller Inc. in New York

Architekt: Alexander Girard, Santa Fé, New Mexico

In Manhattan, 8 East 53rd Street, kombinierte Alexander Girard eine Verkaufsausstellung der (von ihm entworfenen) Herman Miller Collection an Vorhang- und Möbelbezugsstoffen mit einem faszinierenden Angebot kunsthandwerklicher und volkskundlicher Sammelobjekte aus aller Welt. Der Formenreichtum und die leuchtende Farbigkeit dieser Gegenstände sind mit den Textilien zu einem phantasievollen und amüsanten Ensemble verschmolzen. Ganz bewußt wurde bei der Präsentation der Vorhangstoffe darauf verzichtet, regelrechte Fensterdekorationen in simulierten Räumen zu zeigen. Die Textilien sind genauso wie etwa die Beispiele mexikanischer oder peruanischer Volkskunst als dekorative (und zugleich den Ladenraum gliedernde) Ausstellungsobjekte behandelt, als Appell an die Phantasie des Käufers. Diese Absicht ist mit einer ganzen Reihe interessanter und einfallsreicher Details verwirklicht worden.

1. Plan. Key: 1 Entrance, 2 Display area with moveable stools, 3 Three-seater, 4 Reception desk, 5 Adjustable hangers for fabric samples, 6 Display tower, 7 Storage cupboards for textiles samples, 8 Sample area, 9 Hinged display panels, 10 Office area.
2. View through the show window. The general impression is established by the cross stripes of the ceiling lights and the individual hanging fixtures, and by the samples of curtain textiles hanging from the ceiling in various colours, lengths, breadths and degrees of transparency.
3. Side view into the display area. A display fitting made of wire hangs from the ceiling, the round and square stools standing below are covered with samples of upholstery textiles of various colours.
4. The focal point of the entrance area is a Victorian threeseater serving at the same time to display single-coloured upholstery fabrics in bright, solid colours.
5. Poster announcing the opening of the exhibition.

1. Grundriß. Legende: 1 Eingang, 2 Schaufensterzone mit abnehmbaren Ausstellungshockern, 3 Sofa, 4 Empfang, 5 Abnehmbare Stangen zum Aufhängen von Vorhangmustern, 6 Ausstellungsturm, 7 Schränke mit Stoffmustern, 8 Musterabteilung, 9 Schwenkbare Ausstellungstafeln, 10 Bürozone.
2. Blick durch das Schaufenster. Der Gesamteindruck ist bestimmt durch die querlaufenden Leuchtbalken aus Einzelglühbirnen und durch die aufgehängten Vorhangmuster, die in Farbe, Länge, Breite und Transparenz variieren.
3. Seitlicher Einblick in die Schaufensterzone. Von der Decke hängend ein Ausstellungsgerüst aus Draht, darunter runde und rechteckige Hocker, bespannt mit Mustern von Möbelbezugsstoffen in verschiedenen Farben.
4. Blickfang des Eingangsbereichs ist das viktorianische Dreisitzersofa, das zugleich farbkräftige Uni-Bezugsstoffe demonstriert.
5. Plakat zur Eröffnung.

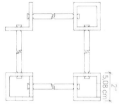

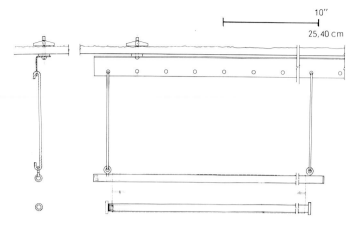

6, 8. The exhibition tower with adjustable poles, pressure-fitted between floor and ceiling (cross-section, see illustration 8) and rods carrying adjustable glass shelves. The view of the underside of the ceiling (illustration 6) shows the alternating sockets for bulbs and the perforated curtain tracks.

7. Section and front view of the L-shaped perforated tracks and the adjustable hangers for fabric samples.

9, 10. At the sample area, the fabric samples are displayed on a double desk covered with fabrics. Like the display stools at the window, it is fitted with round steel legs which are stuck into plugs anchored in the floor.

11. Fabric samples of various sizes and hung one behind the other make an effective composition of planes and volumes. The doors of the storage cupboards (left) are covered with upholstery fabrics.

6, 8. Der Ausstellungsturm, ein Spannstützenregal aus verchromten L- und Vier-kantprofilen (Querschnitt siehe Abb. 8) mit Rundstäben als Auflage für verstell-bare Glastablare. Die Deckenuntersicht in Abb. 6 zeigt die im Wechsel montierten Sockelkästen für die verspiegelten Glühbirnen und die Lochschienen für die Auf-hängung der Stoffmuster.

7. Schnitt und Ansicht der L-förmigen Lochschienen und der variablen Stoffmuster-aufhängung.

9, 10. In der Musterabteilung dient ein stoffbespanntes Doppelpult zur Vorführung von Stoffmustern. Wie die Ausstellungshocker am Fenster ist es mit Stahlrohr-stützen auf fest im Boden eingelassene Zapfen gesteckt.

11. Die in verschiedenen Tiefen des Ladens aufgehängten, verschieden großen Stoffmuster bilden ein reizvolles Spiel aus Flächen und Räumen. Die Türen der Wandschränke mit den Stoffmustern (links) sind mit Polsterstoffen bezogen.

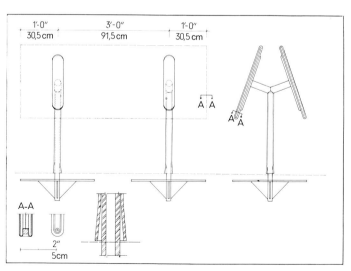

Carpet Showroom in Berne

Designer: Andreas Christen, Zurich

When this showroom of the Berne firm of Max König was redesigned, the problem was to present a collection of 220 different carpet samples in a way that had immediate impact, made effective use of the space available, and allowed for easy supervision by the sales staff. Since there is an unobstructed view into the interior, the showroom had to act as a display window as well. The designer, therefore, developed a type of wall-unit that could be moved wherever it was required. Furthermore, a method of lighting had to be found which was efficient and in which the individual lighting fixtures remained concealed. The carpet samples were put into cylindrical containers made of sheet aluminium, which were fixed to the walls in three rows. The mobile partition walls consist of panes of white, translucent acrylic sheet. Behind these are fluorescent tubes, which produce an even, diffused light.

Ausstellungsraum für Teppiche in Bern

Entwurf: Andreas Christen, Zürich

Bei der Umgestaltung dieses Ausstellungsraumes für die Firma Max König in Bern war eine Kollektion von 220 Spannteppichmustern raumsparend und übersichtlich zu präsentieren. Da der Raum von außen einzusehen ist, sollte er zugleich als Schaufenster dienen. Deshalb waren bewegliche Wandelemente zu entwickeln, die sich ohne Mühe umgruppieren lassen. Außerdem mußte eine möglichst intensive Beleuchtung geschaffen werden, ohne daß die Beleuchtungskörper störend in Erscheinung treten durften. Die Teppichmuster wurden in zylindrischen Behältern aus Aluminiumblech untergebracht, die in drei Reihen übereinander an den Wänden befestigt sind. Die beweglichen Trennwände bestehen aus mattweißen, durchscheinenden Acrylglasscheiben, hinter denen Fluoreszenzröhren montiert wurden, so daß diese Leuchtwände ein gleichmäßiges Streulicht geben.

1. View through the display window. Mobile light-screens serve as room partitions. The flat back-lighting they provide gives effective modelling to the objects displayed in front of them.
2, 3. The cylindrical containers made of sheet aluminium are fixed to the back wall by two screws. A spring action locks the carpet into the cylinder so that only one third of it shows. An indent in the baseplate makes it easy to remove the samples which are displayed according to gradations of colour.
4, 5. Side view of one of the mobile partition walls. Back and front made of white translucent acrylic sheet; V-shaped sides of sheet aluminium.

1. Blick durch das Schaufenster. Als Raumteiler dienen mobile Leuchtkästen, deren opalweiße Flächen die davor aufgestellten Gegenstände in starkem Gegenlicht konturieren.
2, 3. Zylindrische Behälter aus Aluminiumblech, an zwei Punkten rückwärts verschraubt, umschließen federnd zwei Drittel der Teppichrollen (70 cm Standardbreite = Zylinderhöhe). Im Bodenblech Einschnitt zum leichteren Herausnehmen der nach Farbstufen geordneten Rollen.
4, 5. Eine der beweglichen Leuchtwände in Seitenansicht. Front- und Rückseite aus weißem, durchscheinendem Acrylglas, V-förmige Seitenbleche aus Aluminium.

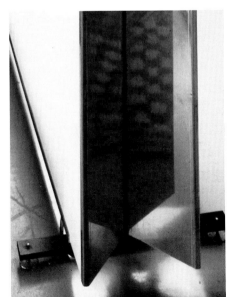

1. Plan. On the left, the light panel.
2. View through the glazed part of the door.
3. On the left, the light panel used for testing the density of the textiles; in front of it, a system of rails with fifty curtain samples. The floor is covered with coconut matting.

1. Grundriß. Links die Leuchtwand.
2. Blick durch den Fensterausschnitt der Tür.
3. Links Leuchtwand mit Tageslichteffekt zur Dichteprüfung, davor Schienensystem mit 50 verschiebbaren Vorhangmustern. Bodenplatte mit Kokosbahnen bespannt.

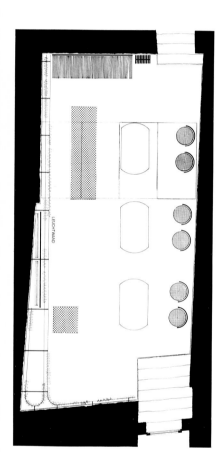

Textile Salesroom in Berne

Architect: Hans Eichenberger, Stuckishaus near Berne

Verkaufsraum für Heimtextilien in Bern

Architekt: Hans Eichenberger, Stuckishaus bei Bern

This original and economical design uses a cellar to enlarge the sales area. The furniture and textile firm of Teo Jakob in Berne was especially fortunate in having at its disposal a vast vaulted cellar, hundreds of years old, which was still in good structural condition. The brickwork and the worn stairs were retained to provide a contrast with the modern textiles. The effect was heightened by the furniture designed by the architect, especially by the black lacquered sample-cupboard, as well as by the hanging spotlights and other lamps which give more diffused beams. Four of them shine on a transverse panel of curtain fabrics stretched over a metal frame.

Bei dieser Lösung wurde auf ebenso originelle wie sparsame Weise ein Kellerraum für die Erweiterung der Verkaufsfläche ausgenutzt. Allerdings waren die Bedingungen bei der Firma Teo Jakob, Möbel und Textilien, in Bern insofern besonders günstig, als hier ein jahrhundertealter, in seiner architektonischen Substanz gut erhaltener, weitgespannt überwölbter Keller zur Verfügung stand. Das Mauerwerk, das Backsteingewölbe und die ausgetretenen Treppenstufen blieben unverändert und bilden einen wirkungsvollen Kontrast zu den modernen Textilien, die hier vorgeführt werden. Den gleichen Effekt bewirken das vom Architekten entworfene Mobiliar, insbesondere der schwarz lackierte Musterschrank, und die Lampen: von der Decke hängende Breit- und Punktstrahler. Vier von ihnen strahlen auf ein querlaufendes Leuchtband aus Stoffbahnen, die über Metallholmen gespannt sind.

Showrooms of the Furniture Factory, Fritz Hansen in Copenhagen

Architect: Bård Henriksen, Copenhagen

These showrooms are on the second floor of two old buildings in Dronningensgade which are connected by a bridge. Favourable lighting conditions prevail in all of the rooms since they all have windows on two sides. With simple means and on a small budget, the architect succeeded in creating a flexible background for the exhibition of furniture; and easily changed settings for the different areas have been achieved with the aid of unusual decorative devices. All walls and ceilings are white, so that the strong colours of the covering fabrics and curtains show effectively. Grids of wood strips set in front of some of the walls relate to the trellis work of the grids suspended from the ceiling. The room partitions, made of waste material or manufactured parts of furniture, are an original solution.

Ausstellungsräume der Möbelfabrik Fritz Hansen in Kopenhagen

Architekt: Bård Henriksen, Kopenhagen

Die Ausstellungsräume nehmen ein Obergeschoß von zwei alten, durch eine Brücke miteinander verbundenen Gebäuden an der Dronningensgade ein. Alle Räume weisen günstige Lichtverhältnisse auf: Sie haben Fenster an zwei Seiten. Dem Architekten ist es gelungen, mit einfachen Mitteln und verhältnismäßig geringen Kosten einen wandlungsfähigen Hintergrund für die auszustellenden Möbelstücke zu schaffen und in den einzelnen Raumzonen mit nicht alltäglichen Gestaltungsmitteln eine abwechslungsreiche Szenerie zu bilden. Die Wände und Decken sind durchweg weiß gehalten, so daß die starkfarbigen Bezugsstoffe und Vorhänge gut zur Geltung kommen. Vor einzelne Wände wurden Gitter aus Holzleisten gesetzt, die mit frei unter die Decke gehängten Lamellenrosten korrespondieren. Eine originelle Lösung zeigen die Raumteiler, die aus Abfällen oder einzelnen Fertigungsteilen der eigenen Möbelfabrikation bestehen.

1. Various curtains are hung on metal rods suspended at about 6 in below the ceiling. In the foreground, a curtain made of metal strips taken from waste material with round, stamped out holes.
2. Here a white translucent plastic sheet is stretched between the suspended curtain rods. This is done in front of the window wall as well, producing an even distribution of light. In the foreground, a partition made of standard elements of chairs.
3. In front of the rear wall which is covered with white plastic sheet and lit from behind, upright strips in sharp silhouette. Pieces of mirrors are stuck to the wall at left.
4. Suspended sculpture made of steel covers used underneath the seats of chairs.
5. A curtain made of metal strips out of which arms of chairs were stamped.
6. Detail of mirror wall.

1. Etwa 15 cm unter die Raumdecke gehängte Metallschienen dienen zur Befestigung verschiedenartiger Vorhänge. Im Vordergrund ein Vorhang aus Abfall-Blechstreifen mit Stanzlöchern.
2. Zwischen die untergehängten Vorhangschienen ist hier eine weiße durchscheinende Plastikfolie gespannt, ebenso vor der Fensterwand; dadurch gleichmäßige Lichtverteilung. Im Vordergrund Trennwand aus serienmäßigen Stuhlteilen.
3. Senkrechte Leisten bilden vor der mit weißer Kunststoff-Folie bezogenen und von hinten beleuchteten Rückwand eine scharf konturierte Silhouette. An der Wand links aufgeklebte Spiegelstücke.
4. Eine Hängeplastik aus Abdeckblechen eines Stuhlmodells.
5. Ein Vorhang aus Metallstreifen, aus denen Armlehnen ausgestanzt wurden.
6. Detail der Spiegelwand.

Showroom for Furniture and Home Textiles of Messrs. Knoll Associates in Los Angeles

Architects: Knoll Planning Unit

With this design for the Knoll establishment in Los Angeles, the firm's own planning unit tried to create an area of special interest at the centre of the showrooms which would effectively attract the attention of the passer-by. They did this by means of a canopy construction with a white square vaulted ceiling; the sides of each bay are 10 ft long and nine ceiling bays cover a floor area of 30×30 ft. The central area was featured as a fountain pool around which tubs with ferns are grouped. The intervals between the thin canopy supports of square-sectioned steel tube are filled with white varnished screens made transparent with punched holes. These help to define smaller areas of display without obstructive views of the showroom as a whole.

Ausstellungsraum für Möbel und Heimtextilien der Knoll Associates in Los Angeles

Architekten: Knoll Planning Unit

Beim Entwurf für die Knoll-Niederlassung in Los Angeles versuchte die firmeneigene Planungs-abteilung im Zentrum der Ausstellungsräume einen Akzent zu schaffen, der die Blicke der an den Schaufenstern vorbeigehenden Passanten in besonderem Maß auf sich ziehen sollte. Dieses Ziel wurde durch den Einbau einer Baldachinkonstruktion mit weißen, quadratischen Deckenschalen von 10 Fuß Seitenlänge erreicht. Die neun Deckenfelder überspannen eine Grundfläche von 30×30 Fuß. Das Feld im Zentrum wurde als Wasserbassin ausgebildet, in dem einige Pflanzenkübel mit Farnkraut aufgestellt wurden. Zwischen den dünnen Stützen aus Vierkantstahlrohr, die die Baldachin-decke tragen, sind einzelne durchsichtige, weiß lackierte Wandschirme mit eingestanzten Löchern gespannt, die kleinere Ausstellungssektoren markieren, ohne daß deshalb die Übersicht über den Gesamtraum verlorenginge.

1. View through the display window towards the vaulted pavilion, the floor of which is covered with a deep pile carpet, while the border areas are finished in parquet flooring. In the background a partition wall of a strong single colour.

2. In the department for outdoor furniture, primary colours – red, blue and yellow – combine with potted plants, a photomural of flying gulls, curtains resembling fishing nets and with strong sun-and-shadow lighting (using spotlights) to create a gay holiday atmosphere.

3. Samples of curtain fabrics are stretched in moveable frames of ceiling height. Each pattern is presented in one or two frames of full height while smaller cuttings show the remaining colours of the respective pattern.

4. The pavilion with the canopies seen from the side. At right, the display window front, at left, the coloured rear wall. Viewed obliquely the perforated screens produce the impression of a closed surface.

1. Blick durch die Schaufenster auf den Baldachinpavillon, dessen Grundfläche mit einem hochflorigen Spannteppich ausgelegt ist, während die Randbereiche einen Parkettfußboden haben. Massive Trennwand im Hintergrund in kräftiger Unifarbe.

2. In der Abteilung für Möbel, die auch im Freien zu verwenden sind, schaffen die Grundfarben Rot, Blau und Gelb zusammen mit Büschen in Pflanzenkübeln, einem Photowandbild fliegender Möven, an Fischernetze erinnernden Stores und einer stark schattenbildenden Beleuchtung mit Punktstrahlern eine heitere Ferienstimmung.

3. Mustercoupons von Gardinenstoffen sind auf raumhohe, bewegliche Rahmen gespannt, wobei jeweils ein oder zwei Rahmen eine Probe in voller Höhe geben, während zusätzliche Rahmen kleinere Abschnitte in den verschiedenen anderen Farbstellungen eines Dessins zeigen.

4. Der Baldachinpavillon von der Seite gesehen. Rechts die Schaufensterfront, links die farbige Rückwand. In der Schrägansicht schließen sich die durchbrochenen Wandschirme zur geschlossenen Fläche.

**Showrooms of Messrs. Knoll International
GmbH. in Düsseldorf and Stuttgart**

Architects: Knoll International Planning Unit

The showroom at Düsseldorf, Berliner Allee, which Messrs. Knoll International have rented together with Messrs. Braun AG. occupies the ground floor of a square pavilion in a new bank building.
All four sides (two on the street front, two on the passage side) have continuous floor-to-ceiling display windows. The two partners (Knoll: furniture and home textiles; Braun: electric musical,
kitchen and household equipment) wanted a solution that would enable each of them to show their
whole production programme without destroying the flowing continuity of the various spaces.
Furthermore, the possibility of varying the sequence of rooms as well as the spatial effects had to be
guaranteed. In spite of the large area occupied by the show windows, it was requested that special
smaller displays of a more intimate character should be possible, if wanted.

**Ausstellungsräume der Knoll International
GmbH. in Düsseldorf und Stuttgart**

Architekten: Planungsabteilung Knoll International

Der Ausstellungsraum, den die Knoll International zusammen mit der Braun AG. in der Berliner
Allee gemietet hat, nimmt das Erdgeschoß eines quadratischen Pavillons im Neubau der Düsseldorfer Stadtsparkasse ein. Alle vier Seiten (zwei Seiten Straßenfront, zwei Seiten in der Passage)
haben durchgehende raumhohe Schaufenster. Es war eine Lösung zu finden, bei der die beiden
Partner ihr Produktionsprogramm (Knoll: Möbel und Heimtextilien; Braun: Elektrogeräte für Musik-
übertragung, Küche und Haushalt) jeweils als geschlossene Einheit zeigen können, die aber auch
fließende Übergänge zwischen den Raumteilen zuläßt. Ferner waren Möglichkeiten für eine Variation
der Raumfolgen und Raumwirkungen zu schaffen. Trotz der sehr großen Schaufensterfläche sollte
es möglich sein, einzelnen Bereichen eine intimere Abgeschlossenheit zu geben.

1. View from the entrance into the common reception room; right, the Knoll exhibition area, left, the Braun AG. department. The floor of the reception zone is covered with grey marble tiles, the rest with brown nylon carpet. Behind the reception table, the central area with walls covered with fabric; the storeroom, tea-kitchen etc. lie behind.
2. Based on the module of 87.5 cm ($34^1/_2$ in) which is valid for the whole building, a ceiling grid (white finished wood frame) was suspended under the structural ceiling (white, light metal construction with lighting fixtures mounted flush with the ceiling). Partition walls, about $34^1/_2$ in wide can be fixed with screws under the grid ceiling.
3. Vertical louvres are provided along the whole front of the display windows so that any part of the window can be totally or partially closed.
4. Street front of display windows.

1. Blick vom Eingang in den gemeinsamen Empfangsraum; rechts der Ausstellungsteil Knoll, links die Abteilung der Braun AG. Fußboden im Empfangsbereich graue Marmorfliesen, sonst brauner Perlon-Velour. Hinter dem Empfangstisch die Kernzone mit festen, stoffbespannten Wänden, hinter denen Abstellräume, Teeküche usw. liegen.
2. Ausgehend von dem Modul von 87,5 cm, der für das ganze Gebäude gilt, wurde unter die bauseitige Decke (weiße Leichtmetalldecke mit bündig eingelassenen Leuchtwannen) eine Rasterdecke abgehängt (Holzkonstruktion, mit weißer Folie belegt). Mit Stellschrauben können Trennwände von 87,5 cm Breite unter die Rasterdecke gespannt werden.
3. Entlang der gesamten Schaufensterfront sind vertikale Lamellenstores gespannt, mit denen sich beliebige Partien der Fenster ganz oder teilweise schließen lassen.
4. Die Schaufensterfront an der Straße.

5. Detail of a corner of a show window with adjustable louvres of white water-proof material.
6. View under the ceiling. Below the original structural ceiling of the room, the wood grid ceiling which was subsequently added. At its lower edge, tracks for separating curtains or adjustable partition walls These partitions are either covered with white or coloured fabrics or panelled in wood. General lighting by lighting fixtures fitted into the structural ceiling; additional reflectors and spotlights can be mounted anywhere on the grid ceiling.

5. Eckdetail am Schaufenster mit den verstellbaren Lamellenstores aus weißem, imprägnierten Gewebe.
6. Deckenuntersicht. Unter der ursprünglichen Raumdecke die nachträglich eingebaute Holzrasterdecke. An ihrer Unterkante Gleitschienen zum Einsetzen von Trennvorhängen oder verstellbaren Trennwänden, die mit weißer Folie belegt, holzfurniert oder mit farbigem Stoff bespannt sind. Grundbeleuchtung durch die eingebauten Wannen in der Raumdecke; zusätzliche Strahler und Spots lassen sich an beliebigen Stellen der Rasterdecke einsetzen.

7. Owing to the fact that the Stuttgart showrooms of Messrs. Knoll International are installed on the upper floor of an industrial building, a series of structural details had to be eliminated when the building was remodelled. In particular the transverse concrete transoms which broaden towards the supporting columns had to be made less conspicuous. This was achieved by means of a suspended grid ceiling made of white varnished wooden rings about 23 1/2 in across. It runs as a broad band down the length of the room. Reaching down to the lower edge of the concrete transoms, it compensates for the predominance of their transverse emphasis. A series of perforated partitions arranged parallel to the transom and made up of upright white varnished wood strips divide the room into different areas.

7. Da die Stuttgarter Ausstellungsräume von Knoll International im Obergeschoß eines Industriebaus untergebracht sind, mußten bei der Neugestaltung eine Reihe unschöner Baudetails zum Verschwinden gebracht werden; insbesondere sollten die querlaufenden, zu den Stützen hin sich verbreiternden Betonunterzüge optisch zurücktreten. Dies wurde mit Hilfe einer abgehängten Rasterdecke aus weißlackierten Holzringen von etwa 60 cm Durchmesser erreicht. Sie verläuft als breites Band in der Längsrichtung des Raumes. Da sie bis zur Unterkante der Betonträger heruntergezogen ist, gleicht sie deren starke Querbetonung aus. Eine Reihe von durchbrochenen Trennwänden aus senkrechten, weißlackierten Holzleisten, die parallel zu den Unterzügen gesetzt wurden, gliedern den Raum in einzelne Bereiche.

1. Entrance area with the oak-pannelled false ceiling, which extends outside the shop and acts as a canopy for the entrance and the display window. The area to the left of the partition has cylindrical lamps hanging from a ceiling of normal height. The false ceiling has rows of built-in spotlights. Materials: floor of red vitrified tiles; walls: whitewashed brickwork or oak strip panelling; structural concrete pillars clad with grey marble.

1. Eingangsbereich mit heruntergezogener Eichenholzdecke, die als Baldachin über Eingang und Schaufenster auskragt, deckenbündige Punktleuchten. Links vom raumteilenden Lattenschirm der Bereich mit voller Deckenhöhe und zylindrischen Pendelleuchten. Materialien: Fußboden rote Klinkerplatten, Wände weiß verputzter Backstein oder Verschalung aus Eichenholzriemen, Betonpfeiler mit grauem Marmor verkleidet.

Furniture Shop in Copenhagen

Architect: Jørgen Bo, Copenhagen

The Westminster Møbelmagasiner showrooms are on the ground floor of a new building in the Frederiksberg Allé; they occupy an area of about 1,400 sq ft. The designer's chief aim was to create an architectural framework of great simplicity, using relatively coarse-textured materials to emphasize, by contrast, the craftsmanship and finish of the furniture on display. A false ceiling and two screens, one solid, the other a latticework of short wooden slats, make it possible for the sizes and lighting systems of the individual room groupings to be changed at will. Consequently, several different furniture arrangements can be displayed simultaneously, without risk of destroying each other's impact.

Möbelgeschäft in Kopenhagen

Architekt: Jørgen Bo, Kopenhagen

Die Verkaufsräume der Westminster Møbelmagasiner in der Frederiksberg Allé nehmen im Erdgeschoß eines Neubaues eine Fläche von rund 130 m² ein. Dem Entwerfer ging es vor allem darum, die Linien des architektonischen Rahmens ziemlich streng zu führen und nüchterne Flächen in verhältnismäßig grobem Material zu schaffen, vor denen sich die ausgestellten Möbel durch die Feinheit ihrer Verarbeitung und ihrer glatten Oberflächen effektvoll abheben. Mit Hilfe zweier Schirmwände – einer geschlossenen und einer transparenten, aus kurzen Latten zusammengesetzten – und durch Einziehen einer untergehängten Decke wurde eine Folge von unterschiedlichen Raumteilen und -höhen mit verschiedenen Abmessungen und verschiedenartiger Beleuchtung geschaffen. So können eine ganze Reihe von Möbelgruppen gezeigt werden, ohne daß sich die einzelnen Modelle in der Wirkung gegenseitig beeinträchtigen.

2. Looking in the opposite direction to pl. 1 carpets mark the display areas of different furniture groups.
3. Large areas of various textures serve as backgrounds for the furniture.
4. The decorative open screen made of oak slats.

2. Blick in Gegenrichtung von Abbildung 1. Teppiche markieren die Standorte der einzelnen Möbelgruppen.
3. Großflächige Texturen als Folie für die Möbel.
4. Der dekorative Raumteiler aus Holzleisten.

Showroom for Furniture and Fabrics of Messrs. Hille of London Ltd. in London

Architects: Peter Moro and Partners, London, in cooperation with Robin Day

Ausstellungsräume für Möbel und Textilien der Hille of London Ltd. in London

Architekten: Peter Moro and Partners, London, in Zusammenarbeit mit Robin Day

The new Hille building in Albemarle Street comprises a total area of 10,000 sq ft. The restricted size of the corner site forced the architects to develop a vertical spatial system using six floors including the basement for exhibition purposes with the two top floors as offices. This vertical treatment underlies the architectural character of the whole building: the ground floor is double height and the aluminium mullions stand out in bold relief on the facade. The infilling panels of the glass curtain wall have a silver-grey backing. The free-standing spiral staircase which links the four lower floors provides further vertical emphasis. Very few columns of reinforced concrete are used to support the structural frame. These were left untreated to contrast with the furniture and the fabrics on display.

Das neu erbaute Hille-Haus in der Albemarle Street umfaßt eine Gesamtfläche von rund 930 m². Die geringe Größe des Eckgrundstücks zwang dazu, das Raumprogramm in der Höhe zu entwickeln, und zwar mit sechs Ausstellungsgeschossen (einschließlich den Kellergewölben im Untergeschoß) und zwei Büroetagen (in den beiden obersten Stockwerken). Diese Vertikalgliederung kommt auch in der architektonischen Gestaltung zum Ausdruck: Die Sockelzone hat doppelte Höhe, und bei der Fassade treten die senkrechten Linien der Aluminiumsprossen besonders hervor. Die Brüstungsfelder des Glas-Curtain-wall sind silbergrau hinterlegt. Auch die an Spannseilen aufgehängte, frei im Raum stehende Wendeltreppe zwischen den vier unteren Geschossen betont die Vertikale. Die auf wenige Stützen beschränkte Tragkonstruktion aus schalungsrauh belassenem Beton steht in bewußtem Kontrast zu den ausgestellten Möbeln und Textilien.

1. Showroom on the ground floor of the Hille House. Existing vaulted cellars penetrating beneath the pavement enlarge the display area; painted white, they make an effective background for furniture.
2. Showroom on the second floor. Windows are covered by floor-to-ceiling curtains.
3. Reception area on the ground floor. In the background, at right, the lift and the main staircase in front of it a spiral staircase with teak steps. Steps and handrails are suspended from steel cables.
4. Overall view of the Hille building.
5. The reinforced concrete supporting columns left untreated, and an old rough brick wall painted white produce an effective contrast of materials. The general lighting of the room is complemented by a row of adjustable spotlights.

1. Ausstellungsraum im Untergeschoß des Hille-Hauses. Vorhandene, unter der Straße liegende Gewölbe erweitern die Ausstellungsfläche und bilden, weiß verputzt, einen effektvollen Hintergrund.
2. Ausstellungsraum im zweiten Obergeschoß. Fenster und Brüstungen durch raumhohe Stores verdeckt.
3. Empfang im Erdgeschoß, Rechts hinten Fahrstuhlschacht und Haupttreppenhaus, davor Wendeltreppe mit Teakholzstufen. Stufen und Handlauf an Stahlseilen aufgehängt.
4. Gesamtansicht des Hille-Hauses.
5. Schalungsrauher Beton an der Stütze und alte, weiß getünchte grobe Ziegelwand als Materialkontraste. Normale Raumbeleuchtung ergänzt durch schwenkbare, in einer Linie aufgereihte Punktstrahler.

Furniture Showrooms in Cologne

Architect: Werner Blaser, Basle

Möbelhaus in Köln

Architekt: Werner Blaser, Basel

The Intermöbel showrooms, in an old commercial building on the Kaiser-Wilhelm-Ring, were designed to the firm's range of modern furniture. When the showrooms were rebuilt, the whole of the ground floor was recessed so that the first-floor overhang protects the pavement in front of the wide ceiling-high display window from the weather. The entrance is to the side of the building, opening off an access corridor; the gallery above the display window can be reached by open-tread stairs. Suspended ceiling-panels, rough concrete, pillars and partitions made up of a number of pivot-mounted sections, serve to define the individual display areas. In spite of its considerable depth, the room gives an impression of flowing continuity. Daylight enters through large square ceiling panels, which can also be artificially lit.

Dem konsequent modernen Möbelangebot der Firma Intermöbel entspricht die Gestaltung ihrer Ausstellungs- und Verkaufsräume, die in einem älteren Geschäftshaus am Kaiser-Wilhelm-Ring untergebracht sind. Beim Umbau wurde das Erdgeschoß so weit zurückgenommen, daß die Auskragung der Obergeschosse dem raumhohen Schaufenster genügend Wetterschutz gibt. Der Eingang wurde auf die Seite verlegt und die Empore über der Schaufensterzone durch eine frei geführte Treppe erschlossen. In Reihen angeordnete, drehbare Lamellen und drei aufgehängte, in der Höhe gegeneinander versetzte Deckenfelder gliedern zusammen mit den Sichtbetonsäulen das Lokal, das trotz beträchtlicher Tiefe seine Einheitlichkeit und sein fließendes Raumkontinuum bewahrt. Tageslicht fällt durch rechteckige Oberlichtfelder ein, die aber auch künstlich beleuchtet werden können.

1. The floor-to-ceiling show window allows an unimpeded view of the interior from the street. On the right, the entrance. Under the gallery, the louvred screens set diagonally, with the furniture angled to match.

2, 3. Longitudinal section and plan showing the ceiling panels under the gallery and the suspended ceiling-pieces in the central part of the sales room.

4. Part of the central part of the showroom. Screens of vertical, anodized aluminium panels in different colours. Under the skylight, a corner of the suspended ceiling (wooden frame with inter-changeable panels covered with black wild-silk). Walls and ceilings painted white; tiled floors.

5. Detail with stairs leading up to the gallery. On the wall, a wood sculpture by Werner Blaser.

6. View from the back of the room looking towards the street.

1. Straßenansicht. Ungehinderter Einblick durch raumhohes Schaufenster. Rechts der Eingang. Unter der Empore diagonale Lamellenreihen und entsprechend schräg gedrehte Ausstellungsstücke.

2, 3. Längsschnitt und Grundriß mit Einzeichnung der aufgehängten Deckenfelder im mittleren Ladenteil und der Deckenelemente unter der Empore.

4. Ausschnitt aus dem mittleren Ladenteil. Drehbare Lamellen aus verschiedenfarbig eloxiertem Aluminium. Unter dem Oberlicht Teile eines eingehängten Deckenfeldes (Holzrahmen mit auswechselbaren Platten, die mit anthrazitfarbener Rohseide bespannt sind). Wände und Decken weiß gestrichen, Fußboden mit Plattenbelag.

5. Detail mit Treppe zur Empore. An der Wand eine Holzplastik von Werner Blaser.

6. Blick aus der Tiefe des Raumes zur Straßenfront.

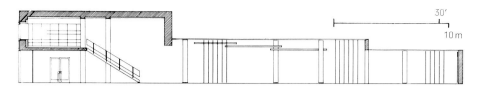

30'
10 m

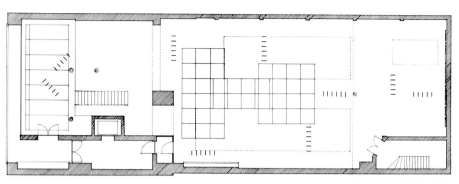

Herman Miller Showrooms in Basle

Architect: Hans G. Walter, Basle

The showrooms for the Herman Miller furniture collection occupy an area of about 3,230 sq ft on the ground floor and basement of a new bank building. The store is in an arcade and its whole front was designed as a display window. The passers-by have an unobstructed view of the interior of the showroom, where three basic materials – wood, marble and curtain fabrics – serve as an unobtrusive background for the display of furniture. The wall to the left of the entrance is faced with 13 pivot-mounted panels, approximately 10 ft by 3 ft. Their fronts are veneered with walnut and their backs are painted white. They can either be used to indicate where a given room ends or they can provide a dark or light-coloured background. The end wall of the room is faced with white marble; back-lit white curtains run the length of the right side wall.

Ausstellungs- und Verkaufsräume der Herman Miller AG in Basel

Architekt: Hans G. Walter, Basel

Die Ausstellungsräume für die Herman Miller Collection nehmen je 150 m² im Erd- und Untergeschoß eines neuen Bankgebäudes ein. Die Front des Geschäftes, das an einer Passage liegt, ist als Schaufenster ausgebildet und gibt den Blick ins Innere frei, wo drei Grundmaterialien – Holz, Marmor und Vorhangstoffe – als Hintergrund für die ausgestellten Möbel verwendet sind. Die Wand links vom Eingang ist mit 13 schwenkbaren Tafeln von 312×85 cm verkleidet, deren Vorderseite mit Nußbaum furniert und deren Rückseite weiß gestrichen wurde. Durch Querstellen der Tafeln lassen sich Raumbegrenzungen andeuten, durch Schwenken um 180° ein heller oder dunkler Hintergrund schaffen. Die Rückwand des Raumes besteht aus weißem Marmor, während die Seitenwand rechts von weißen, von rückwärts beleuchteten Vorhängen eingenommen wird.

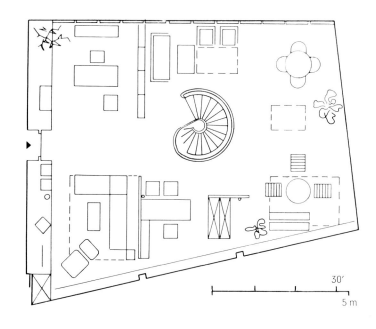

1. Ground-floor showroom seen from the entrance. In the centre, the spiral staircase to the basement. End wall of white marble. Daylight enters the room through six 2 ft cylinders set in the grey painted ceiling.
2, 3. Plans of the ground floor (above) and the basement.
4. View of the display windows facing the arcade.
5. Some of the pivot-mounted panels to the left of the entrance on the ground floor. One of the panels has been reversed to show its white side.
6. The back-lit curtains which run along the right wall.

1. Blick vom Eingang her in den Ausstellungsraum im Erdgeschoß. In der Mitte die Rundtreppe zum Untergeschoß. Rückwand weißer Marmor. Durch sechs etwa 60 cm hohe Zylinder in der grau gestrichenen Decke fällt Tageslicht ein.
2, 3. Grundriß von Erdgeschoß (oben) und Untergeschoß.
4. Blick auf die Schaufenster an der Passage.
5. Einige der schwenkbaren Wandtafeln vor der linken Seitenwand im Erdgeschoß. Eines der Felder ist um 180° gedreht, so daß der weiße Anstrich sichtbar wird.
6. Die von rückwärts beleuchtete Vorhangwand an der rechten Längsseite.

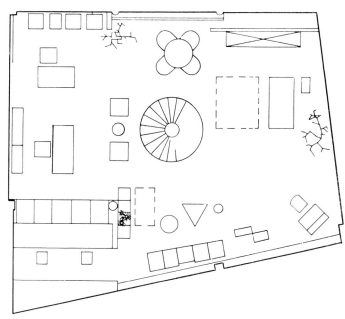

7. An elegantly curved spiral staircase leads to the basement, where the planning and model construction departments are located. The light construction of this staircase, and its central position, allow the customer to survey the objects on display in the farther room while descending the stairs.

8. One of the basement walls has ten recesses, with indirect top-lighting, in which various types of chairs are displayed.

7. Eine zügig geschwungene Wendeltreppe führt ins Untergeschoß, wo auch die Abteilung für Planung und Modellbau untergebracht ist. Durch die leichte Konstruktion der Treppe und ihre zentrale Lage hat der Kunde schon während des Hinuntersteigens einen Überblick über die Ausstellungsobjekte dieses zweiten Raumes.

8. In einer Wand des Untergeschosses sind zehn von oben durch Leuchtfelder erhellte Nischen eingebaut, in denen verschiedene Stuhltypen gezeigt werden.

9. An illuminated screen (left) is used to test the translucency of curtains. These are hung behind the slightly protruding wall when not in use, and are drawn in front of the screen by pulleys for customers. An enlarged photograph on the back wall gives the room additional depth. Ceiling lights were dispensed with. Spotlights, table-lamps and floor lamps dramatically isolate the furniture arrangements.

9. Eine Leuchtwand (links) bietet die Möglichkeit, Vorhänge auf ihre Lichtdurchlässigkeit zu testen. Sie hängen normalerweise verdeckt hinter der etwas vorspringenden Wand und werden zur Vorführung an Schienen vor den Leuchtschirm gezogen. Auf Deckenleuchten ist verzichtet. Spots, Tisch- und Stehlampen setzen die nötigen Akzente. Eine Großphotographie an der Rückseite erweitert optisch den Raum.

Lamp Shop in Milan

Architect: Vittoriano Viganò, Milan
Lighting Fittings: Gino Sarfatti

Arteluce occupies five storeys of an old building on the Via Spiga. The upper basement and the ground floor serve as show rooms, the lower basement as a store, while the mezzanine and the first floor house the administration and the management. By setting the front of the shop back slightly, a covered entrance hall was achieved. From the central window next to the entrance, one can look down through a well of about 10 × 13 ft into the basement. The appeal of this front part of the shop lies in its spatial relationships and the strong modelling of the wall panels. In the rear, the plastic form of the spiral staircase is seen against the emphatic horizontal line of the mezzanine, which has no balustrade.

Lampengeschäft in Mailand

Architekt: Vittoriano Viganò, Mailand
Beleuchtungstechnik: Gino Sarfatti

Die Mailänder Niederlassung der Firma Arteluce nimmt fünf Geschosse eines alten Gebäudes in der Via Spiga ein: Das erste Untergeschoß und das Erdgeschoß dienen als Ausstellungsräume, das zweite Untergeschoß als Lager, während ein Zwischenstock und das erste Obergeschoß Verwaltung und Geschäftsleitung aufnehmen. Im Erdgeschoß wurde die Ladenfront etwas zurückgenommen, so daß eine überdeckte Vorhalle entstand. Vom Mittelfenster neben dem Eingang aus sieht man durch einen 3 × 4 m großen Schacht hinunter in den Ausstellungsbereich des Untergeschosses. Die räumlichen Überschneidungen, die sich dabei ergeben, und die kräftige Reliefierung durch plattenförmige Wandelemente machen den Reiz dieses vorderen Ladenteils aus, während die rückwärtige Zone ihr Gepräge durch die expressive Plastizität der Wendeltreppe und des geländerlosen Zwischengeschosses erhält.

1. View over the well from the display window next to the entrance. The staircase provides a strong plastic element. It leads to the administration office on the first floor; the open mezzanine serves as landing.
2. Night view of the ground floor.
3. View through the display window down into the showroom in the basement.
4. Plan of ground floor. Key: 1 Entrance hall, 2 Entrance, 3 Well, 4 Staircase to the upper floor, 5 Staircase to the basements, 6 Counter, 7 Display platform.
5. Longitudinal section. Key: 1 Lower basement (storage), 2 Upper basement (display), 3 Ground floor (display), 4 Mezzanine (secretary's office), 5 First floor (administration).
6. View from the rear part of the ground floor towards the entrance of the shop and the balustrade of the well.

1. Blick vom Schaufenster neben dem Eingang über den Schacht hinweg auf die plastisch betonte Treppe zur Verwaltung im ersten Obergeschoß mit dem offenen Zwischengeschoß als Treppenpodest.
2. Ansicht des Erdgeschosses bei Nacht.
3. Blick durch das Schaufenster auf den Ausstellungsraum im Untergeschoß.
4. Grundriß des Erdgeschosses. Legende: 1 Vorhalle, 2 Eingang, 3 Schacht, 4 Treppe zum Obergeschoß, 5 Treppe zu den Untergeschossen, 6 Ladentisch, 7 Ausstellungsplattform.
5. Längsschnitt. Legende: 1 Zweites Untergeschoß (Lager), 2 Erstes Untergeschoß (Ausstellung), 3 Erdgeschoß (Ausstellung), 4 Zwischengeschoß (Sekretariat), 5 Erstes Obergeschoß (Verwaltung).
6. Blick aus dem rückwärtigen Teil des Erdgeschosses auf Ladeneingang und Brüstung des Schachtes.

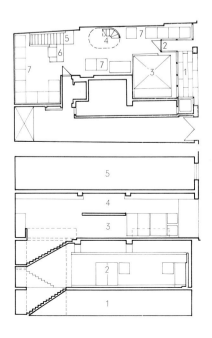

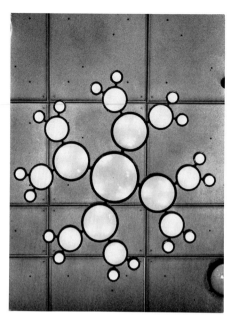

7. View from the well towards the ceiling of the display room on the ground floor.

8. Part of the ceiling which is divided up into a system of moveable panels of different sizes above which the necessary electrical ducts are housed. Each panel can be easily removed to be refitted with new lights.

9. The system of dismountable ceiling panels is complemented by wooden troughs which display built-in ceiling lamps.

10. View into the basement showing the interplay of the uniform, prefabricated display elements. These elements consist of fibreboard panels framed in hardwood. They are available in different sizes (basic module of about $21\frac{1}{2} \times 21\frac{1}{2}$ in), and are applied either to the grid of a suspended ceiling, as wall panelling of different widths and heights, or as platforms suspended just above floor level. Wooden boxes of different sizes and three heights (about $21\frac{1}{2}$, $27\frac{1}{2}$ and $43\frac{1}{2}$ in) display table lamps. This display system enables each article to be shown against an individual background. Concealed ducts for the electric wiring allow an easy exchange of the display articles.

11. The smooth sweeping lines of the spiral staircase, the modelling of the ceiling together with the system of display panels provide an attractive setting which although lively in itself allows the objects on display to play the leading role. Light-coloured plastered walls; display panels in colours of natural wood; grey sisal floor covering.

7. Blick aus dem Schacht gegen die Decke des Erdgeschoß-Ausstellungsraumes.

8. Ausschnitt aus der Decke, die in ein System von beweglichen Platten in verschiedenen Größen unterteilt ist, über denen die erforderlichen elektrischen Leitungen liegen. Jede Platte kann mit wenigen Handgriffen abgenommen und mit neuen Lampenmodellen bestückt werden.

9. Das System der demontablen Deckenplatten wird durch Holzkästen zur Demonstration von eingebauten Deckenleuchten ergänzt.

10. Blick in das Untergeschoß, der das Zusammenspiel der gleichartigen, vorgefertigten Ausstellungselemente deutlich macht. Diese Elemente bestehen aus Holzfaserplatten mit Hartholzprofilen als Einfassung; sie sind in verschiedenen Größen vorrätig (Grundmodul 55×55 cm) und werden entweder als untergehängte Rasterdecke, als Wandverkleidung mit unterschiedlichen Breiten- und Höhenmaßen oder als knapp über dem Boden schwebende Plattformen verwendet. Zur Demonstration von Tischlampen werden Holzkästen in verschiedenen Größen und drei Höhen (55, 70, 110 cm) eingesetzt. Dieses System ermöglicht es, jedes einzelne Ausstellungsstück vor einem eigenen Hintergrund zu zeigen, wobei verdeckte Leisten für die elektrische Stromführung einen leichten Wechsel gestatten.

11. Großflächige plastische Volumen wie die Betonblenden der Wendeltreppe und die Deckenprofile ergeben mit dem System der Ausstellungstafeln ein einheitliches Gesamtbild, das bei aller Expressivität sich doch dem Ausstellungsgut unterordnet. Wände hell verputzt, Ausstellungsplatten Naturholzton, Fußboden grauer Sisal.

Lamp Shops in Rome and Milan

Architects: Gian Antonio and Emiliano Bernasconi, Milan

Lampengeschäfte in Rom und Mailand

Architekten: Gian Antonio und Emiliano Bernasconi, Mailand

For the display and sale of Stilnovo wall, ceiling, and table lamps, the architects developed a system of elements which could be adapted to shops of every sort of ground plan and size. To display wall lamps, they designed plastic-faced wall panels in various sizes which are suspended between steel $\underline{I}$ section supports, extending to full ceiling height. Suspended ceilings, with wooden frames and sound absorbent fillings, house all necessary electric installations – in the same way as the wall panels do – and serve to display ceiling lamps. Standard lamps are displayed either in front of white painted plastered panels, mirror walls, or wood veneered wall partitions.

Für die Ausstellung und den Verkauf von Wand-, Decken- und Tischleuchten der Firma Stilnovo entwickelten die Architekten ein System von Elementen, die für verschiedene Läden mit beliebigen Grundrissen und Dimensionen verwendet werden können. Zur Vorführung von Wandleuchten entwarfen sie kunststoffbeschichtete Wandtafeln in verschiedenen Größen, die zwischen raumhohen Eisen-Spannstützen mit $\underline{I}$-Profil eingehängt werden. Zur Präsentation von Deckenleuchten dienen Unterdecken aus Holzrahmen mit schallschluckenden Füllungen, in die ebenso wie bei den Wandfeldern alle notwendigen elektrischen Installationen eingelassen sind. Stehlampen werden meist vor weißen Putzflächen, Spiegelwänden oder Wandteilen mit Holzfurnier gezeigt.

1. The Stilnovo shop at the Via Due Macelli in Rome consists of a sequence of rooms of different sizes, a dark stripe on the marble floor marks the longitudinal axis. Arches of different widths link the individual rooms and are the dominating motive of the design.
2. The front part of the Stilnovo shop in the Via Turati, Milan, rises two storeys. The supports of the wall panels are correspondingly high. In the background, the inserted gallery.
3. Mirror walls make the room seem larger and appear to multiply the lamps which are suspended at random. They are also reflected by the polished marble floor.
4. At the centre of the room, the platform of the gallery is supported by a large column clad in aluminium.

1. Das Stilnovo-Geschäft an der Via Due Macelli in Rom besteht aus verschieden großen, hintereinandergereihten Räumen, wobei ein dunklerer Streifen im Marmorfußboden die Längsachse betont. Dominierendes Motiv sind die unterschiedlich breiten Arkadenbögen, welche die Räume verbinden.
2. Der Stilnovo-Laden an der Via Turati in Mailand reicht in seinem vorderen Teil durch zwei Geschosse. Die Eisenträger der Wandtafeln haben eine entsprechende Höhe. Im Hintergrund das eingesetzte Galeriegeschoß.
3. Spiegelwände erweitern den Raum und vervielfachen die locker gehängten Lampenmodelle. Auch der Fußboden aus geschliffenem Marmor spiegelt die Beleuchtungskörper.
4. Die Galerie-Plattform wird von der frei stehenden, aluminiumverkleideten Säule in der Raummitte gestützt.

Wine Shop in Milan

Architects: Chini, Gaviglio, Lacca, Milan

When the Vino-Vino shop on the Corso S. Gottardo in the old part of Milan was redesigned, the owners, with only a limited budget at their disposal, wanted their shop to have a pleasant, inviting atmosphere, and to be able to present their rich assortment of Italian and foreign wines to a rather demanding clientele in an unusual and elegant manner. The height of the room was reduced by means of a false ceiling of acoustic tiles, and its apparent depth increased by placing a large window in the end wall to allow an unobstructed view of the adjoining store-room. The former bar was retained as a wine-tasting counter and the right half of the all-glass front was designed as a recess with two separate entrances. For the bottle-racks see pl. 6 and 7.

Wein- und Spirituosenhandlung in Mailand

Architekten: Chini, Gaviglio, Lacca, Mailand

Bei der Modernisierung des Ladenlokals der Firma Vino-Vino am Corso S. Gottardo in der Mailänder Altstadt sollte der bisherige Ausschank in Form einer Probierbar erhalten bleiben, zugleich war mit begrenztem Budget eine einladende Atmosphäre zu schaffen. Sie sollte einer anspruchsvollen Kundschaft das reichhaltige Sortiment an in- und ausländischen Spitzenweinen auf nicht alltägliche, möglichst elegante Weise präsentieren. Zunächst wurde die Raumhöhe durch Einziehen einer Zwischendecke aus schallschluckenden Gipsplatten reduziert. Die Betonung der Raumtiefe, die sich dabei ergab, erfuhr eine weitere Verstärkung durch das große Fenster, das den Durchblick in den anschließenden Lagerraum freigibt und so die Verkaufszone optisch erweitert. Die Ganzglasfront bildet in der rechten Hälfte eine Eingangsnische mit zwei Türen. Zur Konstruktion der aus Draht gebogenen Flaschenregale siehe die Abbildungen 6 und 7.

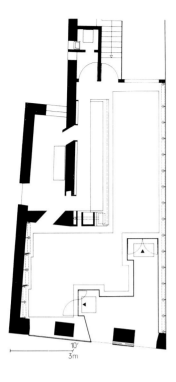

10'
3m

1. In the left-hand part of the store a structural pillar provides the background for a display rack.
2. Ground plan.
3, 4. The sales area and the sampling bar have separate entrances.
5. Overall view. On the right, the open entrance niche; in the background, the window of the storeroom.

1. In der linken Ladenhälfte ist die Glasfront vor den Stützpfeiler gezogen, dessen Vorderfront ein Ausstellungsregal trägt.
2. Grundriß.
3, 4. Verkaufsbereich und zurückgesetzte Probierbar haben getrennte Eingänge.
5. Gesamtansicht. Rechts offene Eingangsnische, im Hintergrund das Lagerraumfenster.

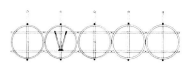

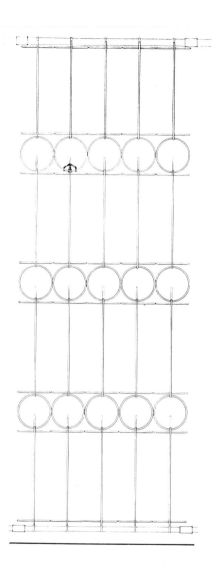

6, 7. For display purposes, low, steel-framed, glass-topped tables and wallracks made of lacquered, welded steel rod are used. The bottles can be displayed either vertically (on removeable steel plates) or horizontally, or any combination of the two. And as the racks themselves are so simple, the bottles become the centre of interest. The tables match the racks in lightness. Fluorescent tubes are mounted in a wooden grid above the racks. Additional overall lighting from square plastic ceiling fixtures.

6, 7. Als Warenträger dienen niedrige Tische mit Eisengestellen und Glasplatten sowie Wandgestelle aus lackiertem Eisendraht, in denen Flaschen vertikal (auf abnehmbaren Blechscheiben) oder horizontal in einer Vielzahl von Kombinationen ausgestellt werden können. Die verhältnismäßig dünnen Drähte, aus denen die Regale zusammengeschweißt sind, ergeben eine ebenso dekorative wie einfache Lösung, die die Flaschen ganz in den Blickpunkt rückt. Dem Filigran der Regale entspricht die Zartheit der Tischgestelle. Über den Regalen liegen Holzkästen mit Leuchtstoffröhren; zusätzliche Raumbeleuchtung durch Deckenfelder mit quadratischen Leuchtwannen aus Kunststoff.

1. View from the street. Brown limestone is used as a facing behind the neon sign. All-glass display window with aluminium coping. Pillars faced with pale grey marble. The passageway behind the smaller freestanding show-case has a Marlux ceiling and wide-beamed lamps. On the right side wall, a sculpture of a turkey, the firm's trade mark, by Alexander Wahl.

1. Straßenansicht. Frontfläche hinter Neonschrift aus bräunlichem Karst. Ganzglasschaufenster mit Aluminiumabdeckung. Säulenverkleidung weißgrauer Marmor. Die Passage hinter der kleineren frei stehenden Vitrine mit Marlux-Leuchtdecke und Breitstrahlern. Schaufensterbeleuchtung Strahler und Spotlights. An rechter Seitenwand Truthahnrelief von Alexander Wahl als Wahrzeichen.

Delicatessen in Vienna

Architects: Karl and Eva Mang, Vienna

The Wild brothers' delicatessen by the New Market is among the best known shops in Vienna. When the old shop was rebuilt, its solid and deliberately traditional character had to be preserved whilst making full provision for personal, strictly Viennese yet quick service. The steel-framed aluminium-faced entrance porch was designed to allow room for a smaller show-case and a passageway besides the two big display windows. Walls and pillars are clad with white and grey marble. The inside of the display window is panelled with walnut, which was also used in the shop itself for the false ceiling and the sales-counters. The sausage and cheese counters, the most important single department, are on the left as one enters the shop.

Delikatessengeschäft in Wien

Architekten: Karl und Eva Mang, Wien

Das Delikatessengeschäft Gebrüder Wild am Neuen Markt gehört zu den bekanntesten Firmen der Wiener Innenstadt. Bei der Modernisierung sollte der solide, traditionsbewußte Charakter des Ladens erhalten bleiben und die Voraussetzung für eine auch weiterhin persönliche, spezifisch wienerische und dabei schnelle Bedienung geschaffen werden. Die Portalkonstruktion, ein Stahlkern mit Aluminiumüberzug, ist so gehalten, daß neben zwei großen Schaufensterauslagen noch eine kleinere Vitrine und eine Passage entstehen. Wände und Pfeiler der Eingangszone sind mit weißem und grauem Marmor verkleidet. Die Innenverkleidung der Schaufenster besteht aus Nußbaumholz, das auch im Laden selbst bei der Hängedecke und den Verkaufspulten verwendet wurde. Die Theken für die Hauptartikel Wurst und Käse sind vom Eingang aus gesehen auf der linken Seite konzentriert; das übrige Angebot erfolgt mit einheitlich gestalteten Gondeln und Regalen.

2, 3. Interior views before and after rebuilding. The shop-fittings dating from about 1900 were replaced by modern cold-storage counters and shelves. The walls and pillars are now covered with charcoal-grey, white and yellow 1½ in square mosaic. Floor of reddish-brown vitrified tiles. False ceiling with walnut panels 2 ft 8 in by 1 ft 4 in. Its shape echoes the former coffered ceiling cherished by the older clientele as a symbol of the traditions of the house.

2, 3. Innenansichten vor und nach dem Umbau. Austausch der um 1900 entstandenen Einrichtung gegen moderne Kühltheken und Regale. Wand- und Pfeilerverkleidung jetzt aus graphitgrauen, weißen und gelben Mosaikplättchen von 4×4 cm. Bodenbelag rotbrauner Klinker. An die bisherige (von den älteren Kunden als Symbol der Geschäftstradition geschätzte) Kassettendecke formal anklingende Hängedecke aus 80×40 cm großen Nußfurnierplatten.

4. Snack bar near the entrance. Walnut-veneered fittings with Formica tops in grey, white or blue, depending on the department. Walnut strip panelling at the back of the display windows can be used to close them off from the rest of the shop.

5. Cheese department cold-storage counter (in front of the cross wall, see pl. 3), at the narrow end of the funnel-like room. The aluminium rack holds the customers' shopping. The room behind the partition walls is used for preparing the goods. There is a lift to the kitchen, the cellar and the subcellar.

6. View from the entrance with its all-glass door. Pillars faced with walnut, aluminium and mosaic. False ceiling in which the lighting fittings (light coffers, wide-beamed lamps and spotlights) as well as the heating and ventilation systems are mounted.

7. Wine department with shelves of bottles.

8. Gondolas and shelves for tinned meat and fish.

4. Imbißecke neben dem Eingang mit Obstgondel. Möbel mit Nußbaumfurnier und Formica-Belägen in Grau, Weiß und Blau zur Kennzeichnung der einzelnen Abteilungen. Wandvertäfelung Nußbaumriemen. Rückseite der Schaufenster mit Jalousetten verschließbar.

5. Kühltheke am Käseverkaufsstand (vor der Querwand, siehe Abb. 3), zu dem hin sich der Raum zwischen den Wurstwarenpulten und den beiden Kassen trichterförmig verengt. Aluminiumroste zum Abstellen von Einkaufstaschen. Hinter Trennwand Vorbereitungsraum mit Aufzug zu Küche, Keller und Tiefkeller.

6. Blick vom Eingang mit Ganzglastür aus. Pfeiler mit Nußbaum-, Aluminium- und Mosaikverkleidung. Holzplatten-Hängedecke mit eingebauter Beleuchtung (Deckenwannen, Breitstrahler, Spots), Heizung und Lüftung.

7. Weinabteilung mit Flaschenstellagen.

8. Verkaufsgondel und Regale für Fleisch- und Fischkonserven.

Hairdressing Salon and Perfume Shop in Varese, Italy

Architects: Cesare Casati and Enzo Hybsch, Milan

By adding a partition of semi-circular units 7 ft 3 in high, the architects transformed an old rectangular shop with a total area of about 800 sq ft into a flowing sequence of spaces. Besides providing an interesting play of convex and concave surfaces, whose relationship change with the position of the observer, the design is extremely functional and makes economical use of the space available. There are four linked areas: a reception area with a perfume shop, a waiting room, a salon, and a cosmetics room. The dominant colours are the white of the roughcast walls and the blue of the glazed ceramic tiles on the floor. A fresco by the Chinese painter Hsiao Chin gives special emphasis to the semi-circular wall behind the waiting-room. Disc-shaped lighting fixtures suspended above the cubicles repeat the circle motif of the whole design.

Friseursalon und Parfümerie in Varese, Italien

Architekten: Cesare Casati und Enzo Hybsch, Mailand

Das langgestreckte Rechteck eines alten Ladenlokals von nur 80 m² Grundfläche gestalteten die Architekten durch Einfügen von 2,20 m hohen, kreisförmigen Zwischenwänden zu einer dynamischen Raumfolge um. Dabei entstand nicht nur ein ästhetisch reizvolles Spiel mit konvexen und konkaven Flächen, deren Überschneidungen von Schritt zu Schritt wechseln, zugleich ergab sich auch eine raumsparende, großzügig wirkende und funktionell gelungene Lösung. Vier Zonen sind geschickt ineinander verzahnt: der Empfangsbereich mit der Parfümerie, der Warteraum, der Damensalon und die Abteilung für kosmetische Behandlung. Das Weiß der Rauhputzwände und das Blau des Fußbodens aus glasierten Keramikplatten sind die beherrschenden Farbtöne. Scheibenförmige Beleuchtungskörper über den Behandlungsnischen nehmen die Kreisform der Grundrißdisposition auf.

1. Textured glass doors and shallow, oval display windows establish the character of the shop from the street. The circular openings in the backs of the show-cases, which allow one to see into the interior of the shop, are an interesting feature of the design.
2. Outline plan.
3. The waiting area. The wall decoration alludes, in linear terms, to the spatial continuity of the various areas.
4, 5. The partition of semi-circular shelf-units acts as an end wall for both the reception area and the perfume shop. The pedestal plates and the front counter panels repeat the circle motif.

1. Türen aus Strukturglas und flache Schauvitrinen mit ovalem Fensterausschnitt bestimmen das Bild der Straßenfront. Originell sind die kreisförmigen Öffnungen in den Vitrinenrückwänden, durch die man ins Innere des Geschäfts sehen kann.
2. Schematischer Grundriß.
3. Die lineare Wanddekoration der Wartezone, ein Fresko des chinesischen Malers Hsiao Chin, nimmt auf das fließende Raumkontinuum Bezug.
4, 5. Empfangszone und Parfümerieverkaufsraum werden rückwärts durch eine Regalwand mit halbkreisförmigen Nischen begrenzt. Sockelplatten und Frontverkleidung der Verkaufstheken variieren das Kreismotiv.

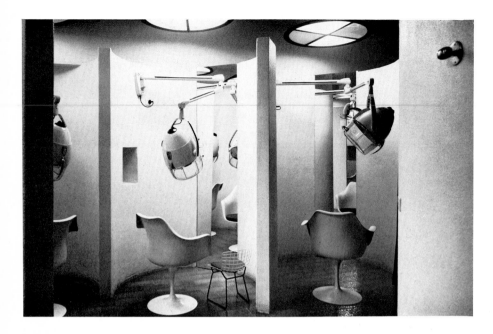

6. Full-length mirrors are fitted flush with the walls of the circular cubicles.

7. The original rectangular shape of the room is still visible above the labyrinth of arcs formed by the 7 ft 3 in high partition walls.

8. View from the waiting room (left) of the washing cubicles.

9. Part of the hairdressing salon. The Knoll International 'tulip' chairs were designed by Eero Saarinen. Handbags, etc. can be left in the rectangular recesses in the cubicle walls. The ceiling lights were designed by the architect himself. Large metal 'collarstuds' placed at random over the walls serve as coat-hooks.

6. In die Wände der kreisförmigen Nischen sind wandhohe Spiegel bündig eingepaßt.

7. Über dem Labyrinth der 2,20 m hohen Zwischenwände aus Kreisabschnitten ist die ursprüngliche rechtwinklige Raumform zu erkennen.

8. Durchblick von der Wartezone (links) zu den Waschkabinen.

9. Ein Ausschnitt aus dem Frisiersalon. Als bewegliche Bestuhlung sind die von Eero Saarinen entworfenen Polyester-Schalenstühle der Firma Knoll International verwendet. Rechteckige Aussparungen in den Nischenwänden dienen als Ablage für Handtaschen usw. Der Entwurf der Lampen stammt von den Architekten selbst. Als Kleiderhaken sind »Kragenknöpfe« aus Metall unregelmäßig über die Wände verteilt.

Perfume Shop and Hairdressing Salon in Zurich

Architect: Francis B. Tamborini, Kloten

Squeezed in between the stair well and another shop, the badly-proportioned rooms presented a considerable problem as far as conversion was concerned. The architect used the horizontal emphasis of funnel shaped lampshades with 3 ft 3 in diameter mahogany frames to give the illusion that the rooms are the same height. The gauze shades produce a soft, flesh-coloured light. The all-glass entrance and the show window give a clear view into the perfumery from the Bahnhofstrasse. The two hairdressing salons behind the perfumery are connected with each other by a corridor; they are uniformly furnished in subtle shades of pale pink. The partitions, which are raised from the floor, the freestanding hair-washing equipment and the cantilevered driers match the clean, functional appearance of the design.

Parfümerie und Friseursalon in Zürich

Architekt: Francis B. Tamborini, Kloten

Eingezwängt zwischen dem Treppenhaus und einem zweiten Lokal boten die verwinkelten, disproportionierten Ladenräume denkbar ungünstige Voraussetzungen für einen Umbau. Mit pilzförmigen Leuchtkörpern aus gazebespannten Mahagonireifen von 1 m Durchmesser sind die unterschiedlichen Raumhöhen einander optisch angeglichen. Es entsteht der Eindruck einer einheitlichen Deckenhöhe, außerdem ergeben die Gazefilter ein weiches, hautwarmes Licht. Durch den verglasten Eingang und das 3 m breite Schaufenster ist der Parfümerie-Verkaufsraum von der Bahnhofstraße her voll einzusehen. Die beiden Coiffuresalons dahinter werden durch einen abgewinkelten Gang verbunden; sie sind einheitlich in zarten Rosatönen gehalten. Vom Boden abgesetzte Zwischenwände, freistehende Apparatursäulen und Trockenhauben an Schwenkarmen fügen sich gut in die rein auf Zweckmäßigkeit und größtmögliche Sauberkeit ausgerichtete Atmosphäre ein.

1, 6. Views of the clinically clean hairdressing salon with its washable, durable surfaces: floor of glass mosaic, partitions of plastic laminate. Instead of normal washbasins there are free-standing hair-washing units: hair driers are equipped with built-in earphones.
2. View from the Bahnhofstrasse. In the window, folding display screens.
3. All-glass entrance wall and display case (right); aluminium-clad door frame.
4. View of the perfume shop. Floor covered with marble aggregate tiles; open shelves with sliding doors, and display tables of mahogany; metal fixtures of polished brass.
5. Ground plan: 1 Entrance, 2 Show window, 3 Perfumery, 4 Hairdressing salon, 5 Connecting passage, 6 W C's, 7 Exit to the store room, the staff rooms and the cloak-room.

1, 6. Zwei Einblicke in den klinisch sauber wirkenden Coiffuresalon aus abwaschbaren, unempfindlichen Materialien: Fußboden aus Glasmarmorsteinchen, Zwischenwände aus Kunststoffplatten. Statt Waschtischen freistehende Apparatursäulen für Wasserzufuhr und -ablauf; in den Trockenhauben sind Musik-Kopfhörer eingebaut.
2. Ansicht von der Bahnhofstraße. Im Schaufenster eine Wechseldekoration mit Paravents.
3. Eingangswand und Ausstellungsvitrine (rechts) in Ganzglaskonstruktion, Türrahmen mit Aluminiumverkleidung.
4. Blick in die Parfümerie. Fußboden aus Eiermarmorplatten, offene Regale mit Schiebetüren und Auslagetische aus Mahagoni, Metallteile aus poliertem Messing.
5. Grundriß: 1 Eingang, 2 Schaufenster, 3 Parfümerie, 4 Friseursalon, 5 Verbindungsgang, 6 Toiletten, 7 Abgang zum Warenlager, zu den Personalräumen und der Garderobe.

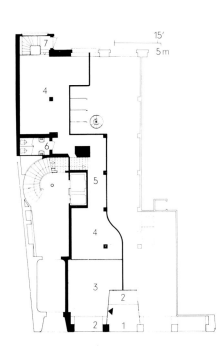

Hairdressing Salon in London

Architects: Gordon and Ursula Bowyer, London
Assistant: Mavis Milburn

This ladies' hairdressing salon is situated just off Oxford Street and has a clientele made up chiefly of models. For this reason, the architects avoided the conventional 'feminine' setting and created instead an atmosphere of cool elegance corresponding to the taste of the clients. Due to the limited space, the various departments were spread over two floors. The main entrance and reception area are on the ground floor; the cloakroom and washing and tinting cubicles are in the basement. For cutting and drying, the customers return to the ground floor, which was designed as one open, unpartitioned area. The floor is of white terrazzo, the ceiling is painted black with a grid of natural pine beams suspended below it. The hessian-covered walls are black in the reception area and dark brown in the drying area.

Friseursalon in London

Architekten: Gordon & Ursula Bowyer, London
Mitarbeiter: Mavis Milburn

Dieser Damensalon, der nahe bei der Oxford Street liegt und dessen Kundschaft sich vorwiegend aus Mannequins zusammensetzt, verzichtet bewußt auf die üblichen femininen Attribute und bietet statt dessen eine Atmosphäre, die in ihrer kühlen Eleganz genau auf den Kundenkreis zugeschnitten ist. Wegen des beschränkten Raumes wurde die Einrichtung auf zwei Geschosse verteilt. Eingang und Empfang liegen im Erdgeschoß; die Garderobe, die Kabinen für Waschen und Färben befinden sich im Untergeschoß. Zum Schneiden und Trocknen geht die Kundin wieder ins Erdgeschoß hinauf, das als offener, nicht unterteilter Raum gestaltet ist. Der Fußboden besteht aus weißem Terrazzo, die Decke ist schwarz gestrichen, darunter hängt ein Gitter aus Kiefernbrettern. Die mit Jute bespannten Wände sind in der Empfangszone schwarz, im Trockenraum dunkelbraun.

1. View from the cutting area on the ground floor looking towards the reception and entrance area. In the foreground, the staircase leading to the basement. The handrails and steps are of teak; the balustrading has panels of Armourplate glass carried on satin-chrome uprights.
2. Exterior view from North Audley Street. The glass shop front is framed in teak. The Armourplate glass entrance door has a centre rail of blue-grey marble, the firm's name is engraved on the adjacent rail of arabescato. There are adjustable vertical blinds behind the main window and adjustable glass ventilation louvres over the entrance door.
3. Plan of ground floor. Key: 1 Reception, 2 Stairs down, 3 Cutting area, 4 Driers.
4. White plastic-covered panels on the walls behind the dressing-tables. There is a recessed mirror with a spotlight mounted above it in every other wall panel. The dressing-table tops are covered with dark grey plastic; their edges, and the storage units underneath, are veneered in teak.
5. View from the drying area towards the cutting area, the reception desk and the entrance. Spotlights mounted on a suspended grid of natural pine beams. In the drying area, hanging lamps with black cylindrical metal shades.

1. Blick von den Frisiertischen im Erdgeschoß auf Empfang und Eingang. Im Vordergrund die Treppe zum Untergeschoß: Handläufe und Stufen aus Teakholz, Füllungen der Balustrade aus Sicherheitsglas zwischen matt verchromten Vierkantsprossen.
2. Außenansicht von der North Audley Street aus. Die verglaste Frontöffnung ist mit einer horizontalen Teakholzschalung umrahmt, in die die Fensterscheibe eingespannt wurde. Die Eingangstür aus Sicherheitsglas hat eine Griffleiste aus blaubeigem Marmor. Ihre Höhe nimmt eine Stoßleiste aus weißem Arabescato mit eingraviertem Firmennamen auf. Hinter dem Hauptfenster sind verstellbare Vertikalblenden montiert, über dem Eingang verstellbare Glaslamellen zur Belüftung.
3. Grundriß Erdgeschoß: 1 Empfang, 2 Treppe zum UG., 3 Schneiden, 4 Trocknen.
4. Im Bereich der Frisiertische sind die Wände mit weißen, kunststoffbeschichteten Platten verkleidet. In jede zweite Wandplatte ist ein Spiegel eingelassen, darüber jeweils eine Punktleuchte. Frisiertische mit dunkelgrauem Kunststoff beschichtet, Kanten und Schrankelemente unter den Tischen aus Teak.
5. Blick vom Trockenraum über die Frisiertische auf Empfang und Eingang. Die abgehängte Gitterstruktur aus Kiefernholz dient zur Befestigung von Punktstrahlern. Im Trockenraum Pendelleuchten mit dunklen Metallzylindern.

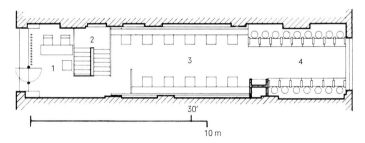

Government Tourist Office in Sydney

Architects: Edwards, Madigan, Torzillo & Partners, Sydney
Design Assistant: Gordon Andrews

When the New South Wales Government rebuilt their Tourist Office on the ground floor of Challis House in Martin Place, all the dividing walls were removed, leaving only the essential supporting pillars. The aim was to create an inviting and impressive public area together with office space sufficient for about 12 desks. The latter form a block on and immediately below the mezzanine. The public area has a gay colourful atmosphere; yet in spite of this visual excitement, it remains simple enough for the passer-by, who has a clear view of the interior through the two glass doorways, to see everything at a glance. The resulting design is extremely functional, spacious, yet entirely sympathetic. The dominant design features are the undulating ceiling with its dramatic lighting, the mosaic floor and the photomontage screens.

Staatliches Reisebüro in Sydney

Architekten: Edwards, Madigan, Torzillo & Partners, Sydney
Mitarbeiter: Gordon Andrews, Designer

Beim Umbau des New South Wales Government Tourist Bureau im Erdgeschoß des Challis House am Martin Place wurden bis auf die unerläßlichen Stützen alle Zwischenwände herausgenommen, um Platz für eine großzügige, einheitliche und funktionsgerechte Lösung zu schaffen. Dabei mußten an den einladend und effektvoll gestalteten Bereich für den Publikumsverkehr Nebenräume für rund 12 Büro-Arbeitsplätze angegliedert werden, die im wesentlichen auf und unter einer Empore zusammengefaßt sind. Der von der Straße her durch zwei verglaste Doppeltüren zugängliche und einzusehende Publikumsbereich zeichnet sich durch eine heitere, farbenfreudige Atmosphäre aus, wobei der Raum bei aller Lebendigkeit klar überschaubar bleibt. Die wichtigsten Gestaltungsmittel sind die Wellendecke mit ihren dramatischen Lichteffekten, der Mosaikfußboden und die Wandschirme mit Photomontagen.

1. View of the public area through one of the glass, bronze-handled double doors. Two free-standing supporting pillars, one with a circular bench, the other with a sculpture by G. Andrews made from old smokestacks, railway tracks, and rusted iron plates. In front of the balustrade of the mezzanine, screens with montages of travel photos extend to the ceiling. Up to table height, they form the fronts of filing cabinets for brochures.
2. Overall view from the mezzanine.
3. Floor plan: Entrances from Martin Place, 2 Lift lobby entrance, 3 Public area, 4 Information desks, 5 Cashier, 6 Advice, 7 Assistant manager, 8 Office, 9 Overseas itineraries, 10 Manager, 11 Photographic murals, 12 Seat, 13 Iron sculpture, 14 Show window.
4. One of the all-glass entrance doors. Marble door surround. Interior wall: vertical cedar battens with brass studs.

1. Blick auf den Publikumsbereich durch eine der Glastüren mit Bronzegriffen. An den frei stehenden Pfeilern rechts eine umlaufende Sitzbank, links eine Eisenplastik aus alten Rauchrohren, Eisenbahnschienen und rostigen Blechen (Entwurf G. Andrews). Vor der Brüstung der Empore in voller Raumhöhe Tafeln mit Photomontagen aus Reisebildern. Bis zu Tischhöhe bilden sie die Fronten von Schubkästen für Prospekte.
2. Übersicht von der Empore aus.
3. Grundriß: 1 Eingänge Martin Place, 2 Eingang Liftvorraum, 3 Publikumsbereich, 4 Auskunftstheken, 5 Kasse, 6 Beratung, 7 Zweiter Geschäftsführer, 8 Büro, 9 Übersee-Reisen, 10 Geschäftsführer, 11 Phototafein, 12 Sitzbank, 13 Eisenplastik, 14 Schaufenster.
4. Eine der Eingangstüren in Ganzglaskonstruktion. Türlaibung Marmor. An der Innenwand Zedernholzleisten mit Messingbeschlägen.

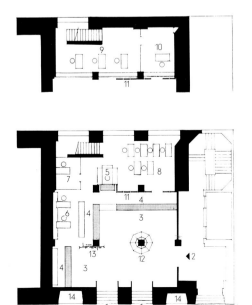

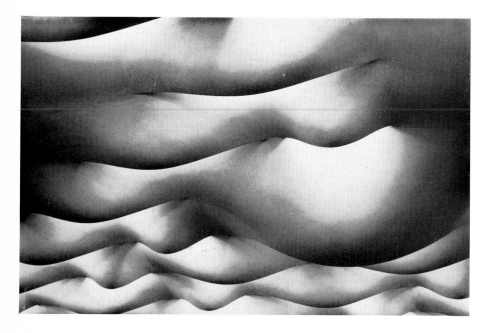

5. The undulating ceiling, made of fibrous plaster, is fixed to a suspended timber grid. For the cowls, only three moulds were sculpted in the workshop and several casts were made of each; each cowl was separately fixed and finished on the site. Neon tubes concealed in the cowls provide strong direct lighting for the photomontage screens and soft overall lighting for the area as a whole.

6. Mosaic floor made of 3/4 in square ceramic tiles of various shades from light grey to coal black.

7. View of the assistant manager's office, with the end of the information desk in the foreground and the cashier's desk on the right.

8. Detail of the public area. Information desks with solid wood or glass tops and funnel-shaped sheet-steel pedestals bolted to the floor. In the actual framework of the desks trays pull out for telephones and card indexes.

5. Die Wellendecke aus Gips mit Fasereinlage ist an einem untergehängten Holzlattengitter befestigt. Für die Mulden wurden in der Werkstatt nur drei Formen vorbereitet, die mehrfach gegossen wurden. Jede Mulde ist einzeln befestigt und erst nach Einbau endgültig bearbeitet worden. In den Wellen sind Glühlampen verdeckt montiert. Dadurch erhält der Publikumsbereich gleichmäßiges, weiches Licht, während die Phototafeln stark angestrahlt werden.

6. Mosaikfußboden aus etwa 2×2 cm großen Keramikplättchen in verschiedenen Farbstufen von Hellgrau bis Anthrazit.

7. Blick über die Informationstheke auf das Büro des zweiten Geschäftsführers; rechts die Kasse.

8. Detailansicht des Publikumsbereichs. Informationstische mit Massivholz- oder Glasplatte und trichterähnlich geformten, in den Boden eingelassenen Stahlblechsockeln. In den Wannen unter den Tischplatten Telephone und Karteien in ausziehbaren Schubkästen.

Pakistan Airlines Ticket Office in New York

Architects: The Space Design Group Inc., New York (Marvin B. Affrime, Director, Frank R. Failla, Associate Designer, Henry F. Kurz, Project Coordinator)

Pakistanisches Flugbüro in New York

Architekten: The Space Design Group, Inc., New York (Marvin B. Affrime, Director, Frank R. Failla, Associate Designer, Henry F. Kurz, Project Coordinator)

An old shop on Fifth Avenue with a plan area of only 36 × 16 ft was at the architects' disposal for the new office of the Pakistan International Airlines. Through the glass facade, recessed three feet from the front face of the building, one has an unbroken view into the interior. The completely symmetrical layout is designed to catch the eyes of passers-by. The intricately interlocking geometric patterns – as well as the layout of the furniture anchored to the floor – are taken from Pakistani art. The light blue of the ceiling, the green of the terrazzo floor, and the deep blue of the polygonal settees, recall the traditional colours of Pakistani ceramic tiles. Light troughs running up the walls or across the ceiling make the room seem larger than it is and are reminiscent of a vaulted mosque.

Für das Büro der Pakistan International Airlines an der Fifth Avenue stand ein altes Ladenlokal von nur 11 × 4,85 m Grundfläche zur Verfügung. Durch eine 90 cm hinter die Gebäudefront zurückgesetzte Glasfassade überblickt man von der Straße aus ungehindert den Raum, der mit seiner symmetrischen Gestaltung als Blickfang für die Passanten konzipiert ist. Aus der pakistanischen Formenwelt sind die sich durchdringenden geometrischen Muster übernommen, in die auch das fest im Boden eingelassene Mobiliar einbezogen wurde. Das Hellblau der Decke, das Grün des Terrazzofußbodens und das Dunkelblau der polygonal geformten Sitzbänke erinnern an die traditionellen Farben pakistanischer Keramikplatten. Senkrechte und quer über die Decke verlaufende Leuchtrinnen weiten optisch den Raum und lassen das Motiv eines Moscheengewölbes anklingen.

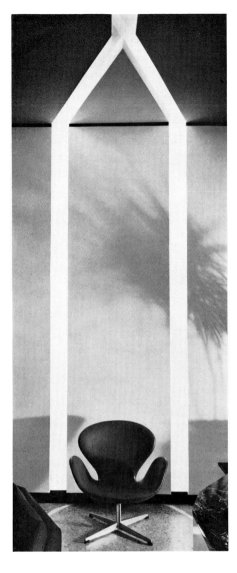

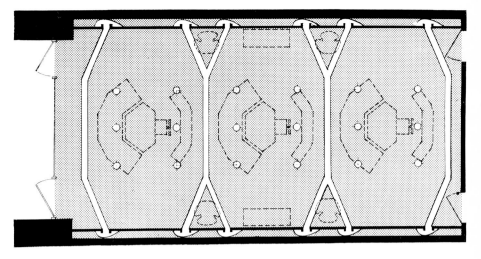

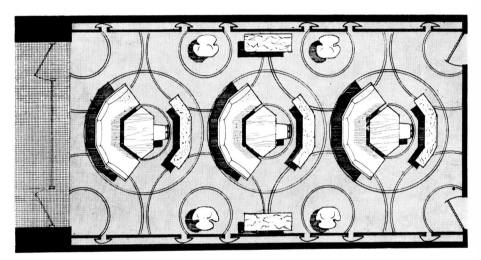

1. The doors of the glass front have anodyzed aluminium frames and handles decorated with inlaid silver which were made by Pakistani artisans, as were the four bronze trays suspended on the walls. On the rear wall, a three-dimensional pattern of teak hexagons which were – like the circle motives of the floor pattern – inspired by old buildings in Lahore.
2. Lighting troughs with concealed light sources. On the walls sprayed cork granules painted white.
3, 4. The ceiling plan and the furniture plan with interlacing geometrical patterns.
5. A ticket unit consisting of a hexagonal teak table, a settee with five seats for customers, and an angled storage unit with black marble top and white plastic-covered sides.

1. In der Glasfront zwei Türen mit Rahmen aus eloxiertem Aluminium, Türgriffe pakistanische Silber-Einlegearbeit. An den Wänden vier Bronzeschalen, ebenfalls pakistanisches Kunsthandwerk. An der Rückwand Relief aus Teakholz-Sechsecken, die ebenso wie die Zirkelmotive des Fußbodens von alten Bauten in Lahore inspiriert sind.
2. Leuchtschlitze mit verdeckten Lichtquellen. An den Wänden weiß gestrichener Korkschrot.
3, 4. Decken- und Möblierungsplan.
5. Ein Buchungsplatz aus Teakholz-Sechsecktisch, fünfsitziger Bank für Kunden und abgewinkeltem Kastenelement mit schwarzer Marmorplatte.

French Central Tourist Office in Zürich

Architect: Francis B. Tamborini, Kloten

An enormous amount of material, tens of thousands of brochures, hotel price lists, forms, posters, photographs and films, had to be stored in a very small space, and in a way that was architecturally effective. So that all the material should be easily accessible, double-sided racks, mounted on ball-bearing pivots (later patented), were devised. They allowed space for four times the number of brochures usually stored. The racks are placed at a comfortable height and under each unit there is a small set of drawers, containing detailed information on hotel prices, etc. The shelves and the drawers are veneered in zebra wood, which was also used for the counters.

Reisebüro der französischen Fremdenverkehrs-zentrale in Zürich

Architekt: Francis B. Tamborini, Kloten

Auf kleinstem Raum war hier eine enorme Dokumentation aus Zehntausenden von Prospekten, Hoteltarifen, Formularen, Plakaten, Photos und Filmen unterzubringen und zudem eine klare architektonische Linie zu finden. Damit das ganze Informationsmaterial übersichtlich zur Hand ist, wurden die Aufbewahrungsmöglichkeiten für Prospekte durch den Einbau von drehbaren, auf Kugellagern montierten (später patentierten) Regalen vervierfacht. Unter jeder Gruppe dieser in bequemer Greifhöhe befestigten Regale befinden sich kleine schwarze Schiebefächer, die zum Arbeiten beliebig herausgenommen werden können und alle zur jeweiligen Prospektgruppe gehörigen Detailinformationen über Hoteltarife usw. enthalten. Für die Verkleidung der Regale und Schiebefächer ist Zebranoholz verwendet, aus dem auch die Theken bestehen.

1. View from the entrance. The counters are set obliquely and are made in two sections, each of a different height, a prerequisite in information offices of this kind. The customer stands and although the information officer stands to serve him, he must also, if necessary, be able to sit and work as at a normal desk. To prevent the counters appearing clumsy, because of their unusual height, the light green carpet was extended over their bases. Counters of zebra wood with white plastic working surfaces; in front, glass panels concealing indirect lighting.
2. Detail of the patented ball-bearing mounted racks.
3. Floor plan.
4, 5. The racks for the posters can be pulled out and spread like fans.

1. Blick vom Eingang her in die Tiefe des Ladenraums mit den schräggestaffelten Theken, die bei Informationsbüros dieser Art unbedingt zwei verschiedene Höhen haben müssen. Der Kunde steht und wird stehend bedient; außerdem soll das Personal aber auch sitzend bei normaler Tischhöhe arbeiten können. Um bei der erforderlichen Höhe ein schwerfälliges Aussehen der Theken zu vermeiden, wurde der hellgrüne Teppich auf einen Sockel hochgezogen und so die Höhe optisch verringert. Theken aus Zebranoholz mit weißen Schichtstoffplatten, Vorderfront Glasplatte mit indirektem Licht zwischen Holz- und Glasplatte.
2. Detailansicht der patentierten, schwenkbaren Regale.
3. Grundriß.
4, 5. Die Halter für Plakate können nach vorn gezogen und fächerförmig ausgeschwenkt werden.

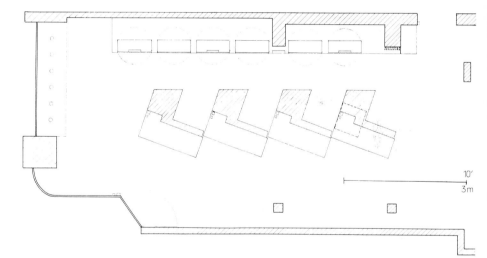

Spanish Tourist Office in Rome

Architect: Julio Lafuente, Rome

The tourist office in the Piazza di Spagna has only a relatively small arcade opening onto the street. In order to gain extra space for the display area and to establish a bay for passers-by, the front was set back to form an open-fronted ante-room; from this an all-glass front wall allows an unimpeded view into the interior. As is frequently the case with tourist information offices, the atmosphere of the country concerned is evoked by the use of characteristic materials and furnishings. The floor covered with p.v.c. tiles is an allusion to the 'Cantorodado' motif of the Spanish patio and the passages leading to the offices are decorated with 'Azulejos' (terracotta) tiles. The niches in the side walls, in which copper and ceramic articles are displayed, are reminiscent of the kitchens of Ibiza. A brick wall demarcates a further office.

Spanisches Reisebüro in Rom

Architekt: Julio Lafuente, Rom

Das an der Piazza di Spagna gelegene Reisebüro hat zur Straße hin nur eine verhältnismäßig schmale Arkadenöffnung. Um Ausstellungsfläche für Vitrinen zu gewinnen und eine Bucht zu schaffen, wurde im vorderen Teil ein allgemein zugänglicher Vorraum abgeteilt, von dem aus eine Ganzglasfront ungehinderten Einblick bietet. Wie häufig bei touristischen Informationsbüros, ist auch hier versucht, durch typische Materialien und Attribute die Atmosphäre des werbenden Landes heraufzubeschwören: Der Fußboden aus Kunststoff-Fliesen läßt das »Cantorodado«-Motiv des spanischen Patio anklingen; »Azulejos«-Kacheln schmücken die Durchgänge zu den seitlichen Büroräumen, und die Nischen in den Seitenwänden, in denen Kupfer- und Keramikgeräte stehen, erinnern an die Küchen auf Ibiza. Eine Ziegelmauer trennt im Hintergrund ein weiteres Büro ab.

1. The entrance is flanked by showcases for exhibiting photopraphs and products of Spanish folk–art, their back walls are hung with hessian. The glass entrance door has a handle of wrought iron (designed by Miguel Ortiz). The doors of the bank of cupboards are splayed to face towards the entrance and serve as panels for posters.

2. Overall view from the ante-room, its floor is finished in the same p. v. c. tiles as the floor of the main office area. On both the right and left they make a stepped joint with the contrasting surface provided by the natural pebbles. The walnut-lined, barrel-vaulted ceiling slopes downwards towards the back of the office to adjust differences in ceiling heights.

3. Longitudinal section and ground-plan. In the section the lower ceiling height of the back part of the room and the transition achieved by the sloping barrel-vaulted, wooden ceiling are clearly shown.

4. View towards the entrance from the central area with its barrel-vaulted ceiling. The fixed panels of the zigzag-fronted cupboards are here faced with walnut strip. On the left, the wall niches lit from above. Overall lighting by ceiling lights and spotlights.

1. Den Eingang flankieren Vitrinen zur Ausstellung von Photos und Erzeugnissen der spanischen Volkskunst. Rückwand mit Hanfmatten bespannt. Glastür mit Griff aus Schmiedeeisen (Entwurf Miguel Ortiz). Die zum Eingang hin gerichteten Türen eines sägeförmigen Schrankes dienen als Plakatwände.

2. Gesamtansicht vom Vorraum aus, der den gleichen Bodenbelag wie der Innenraum hat. Rechts und links treppenartig zurückspringende Fußbodenzone mit Belag aus Kieseln. In der mittleren Zone leitet ein nach hinten niedriger werdendes Tonnengewölbe mit Lattenverkleidung aus Nußbaumholz in den niedrigen rückwärtigen Teil des Empfangsbereichs über.

3. Längsschnitt und Grundriß. Im Schnitt wird die im hinteren Teil niedrigere Raumhöhe und die Überleitung durch die schräge Holztonne deutlich.

4. Blick von der leicht eingeschnürten Mittelzone mit der holzverschalten Tonnendecke zum Eingang. Die Seitenflächen des zickzackförmigen Schrankes sind hier mit Nußbaumleisten verschalt. Links die von oben beleuchteten Wandnischen. Raumbeleuchtung mit Deckenstrahlern und Spots.

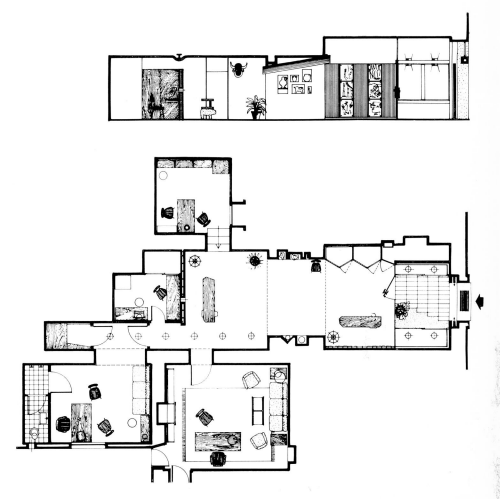

5. The counter to the left of the entrance and the terracotta mural designed by Miguel Ortiz behind it, its motifs are taken from folk art. Both counters (cf. pl. 6) are made of walnut; one side rests on a metal support, the other on an animal-like sculpture in tufa stone.
6. The partition wall in the background is made of flat bricks. On the right, an iron swivel-rack for brochures. The wall of the passage on the left is covered with 'Azulejos' tiling.
7. View from the vaulted area into the back part of the reception zone, which has been given a plain, comparatively low ceiling, so that the visual continuity between the office behind the brick wall and the main reception room is not interrupted.

5. Die Theke links vom Eingang, dahinter farbige Terrakottawand mit Volkskunstmotiven (Entwurf Miguel Ortiz). Die beiden Theken (siehe auch Abb. 6) bestehen aus Nußbaumholz; sie werden auf der einen Seite von einer Metallstütze getragen, mit der anderen ruhen sie auf einem tierähnlichen behauenen Tuffsteinblock.
6. Die Trennwand im Hintergrund aus flachen Ziegeln. Rechts ein drehbarer Prospekthalter aus Eisen. Links ein mit »Azulejos«-Platten verkleideter Durchgang.
7. Blick aus dem Tonnenraum in den rückwärtigen Teil des Empfangsbereichs, der eine gerade, niedriger liegende Decke hat. Die Trennwand reicht nicht bis zur Decke, so daß der dahinterliegende Büroraum optisch noch mit dem Empfangsraum verbunden bleibt.

1. Overall view from Friedensstraße. The all-glass front, the Plexiglas cube, the false ceiling, and the side walls which are suspended between ceiling and the floor, give the room a feeling of lightness and freedom.

1. Gesamtansicht von der Friedensstraße aus. Ganzglasfront, Schriftwürfel, abgehängte Zwischendecke aus stilisierten Flugzeugen, von Decke und Fußboden abgesetzte Seitenwände vermitteln einen Raumeindruck von schwebender Leichtigkeit.

Office of EL-AL Israel Airlines in Frankfurt am Main

Architects: Fautz and Rau, Darmstadt

Flugbüro der EL-AL Israel Airlines in Frankfurt am Main

Architekten: Fautz und Rau, Darmstadt

A former shop on the ground floor of a banking house was converted into a branch office of the Israel Airlines. The comparatively small rooms were made to appear larger by the imaginative arrangement of walls and furniture, and the booking-office was designed to serve as a reception area as well. A white cube made of Plexiglas with EL-AL in black lettering, lit from within, extends through the glass front to catch the eye of the passers-by, even from a distance. The open character of the reception room invites entry. This impression is achieved by the use of a frameless, all-glass front and by the continuation of the pavement into the interior. The false ceiling is made of stylized aeroplanes, and the roughcast side walls and the relief lettering on the rear wall give the room a sturdy rustic character.

Ein früherer Laden war als Zweigstelle der israelischen Fluggesellschaft einzurichten. Dabei mußten die relativ kleinen Räume durch geschickte Anordnung von Wänden und Möbeln optisch vergrößert und das Office für den Publikumsverkehr als repräsentativer Empfangsraum ausgestaltet werden. Ein über die Glasfront hinausragender weißer, von innen beleuchteter Plexiglaswürfel mit dem Signum der Gesellschaft EL-AL in schwarzen Buchstaben zieht schon von weitem die Blicke der Passanten auf sich. In großzügiger Offenheit lädt der Empfangsraum zum Betreten ein. Dieser Eindruck wird durch die völlig rahmenlose Glasfront und das Weiterführen des Bürgersteigpflasters in den Raum hinein erreicht. Die Decke aus stilisierten Flugzeugen, der grobe Putz der Seitenwände und das Schriftrelief auf der Rückwand geben dem Raum eine rustikale Note.

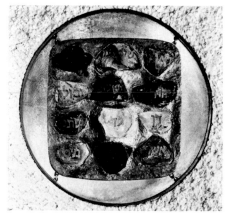

2. Stylized aeroplanes, suspended at two different levels, overlap one another to form a false ceiling. General lighting by concealed lamps mounted between the aeroplanes.

3. Copper bowl framing a much-enlarged breast-plate of a high priest. Instead of precious stones in the colours of the twelve tribes of Israel, pieces of coloured glass are used on which the names of the tribes are engraved.

4. Seating arrangement at the entrance. On the right, the all-glass door with EL–AL in Hebrew on the handle. Cacti and the stylized breast-plate of a high priest.

5. By the all-glass front, a seating arrangement in oak with violet-blue upholstery in sympathy with the general rustic style of the room, which is emphasized by the cobble effect of the floor and the roughcast walls. Cacti in floor-tubs.

2. Als Zwischendecke sind in zwei verschiedenen Höhen sich überschneidende, stilisierte Flugzeuge aufgehängt. Dazwischen hängen verdeckte Strahler, die den Raum ausleuchten.

3. Kupferschale mit stark vergrößertem Brustschild eines Hohepriesters. Statt Edelsteinen in den Farben der 12 Stämme Israels sind Farbglasbrocken mit eingravierten Stammesnamen verwendet.

4. Sitzgruppe am Eingang. Rechts die Nurglastür. Am Türgriff die hebräischen Buchstaben EL-AL, Kakteen und stilisiertes Brustschild des jüdischen Hohepriesters weisen auf das Heimatland der Gesellschaft.

5. An der Fensterfront Sitzgruppe aus Eiche mit blau-violetten Polsterbezügen, angepaßt an die rustikale Gesamtnote, zu der auch Pflasterboden und grober Wandputz beitragen. Bodenschale mit Kakteen.

6. Partition wall with the EL–AL device in relief in
both Hebrew and Roman lettering. The ceiling and
the right wall are continued beyond the cross wall,
in order to increase the depth of the room. The furniture was designed by the architects.
7. Floor plan. Key: 1 Entrance, 2 EL–AL cube, 3 House
entrance, 4 Offices, 5 Desk, 6 Counter, 7 Seats,
8 Poster display, 9 Brochure rack, 10 Telephone-
box, 11 Scales, 12 Luggage, 13 Telex room, 14
Booking-office, 15 Passage, 16 Office.

6. Die Trennwand mit Schriftrelief aus hebräischen
und lateinischen EL-AL-Buchstaben. Decke und
rechte Wand laufen Tiefe schaffend über die Querwand weiter. Mobiliar Architektenentwurf.
7. Grundriß. Legende: 1 Eingang, 2 Leuchtwürfel,
3 Hauseingang, 4 Office, 5 Schreibtisch, 6 Stehpult,
7 Sitzgruppe, 8 Plakatauslage, 9 Prospektauslage,
10 Telefonbox, 11 Waage, 12 Gepäck, 13 Telex-Raum,
14 Buchungsbüro, 15 Gang, 16 Büro.

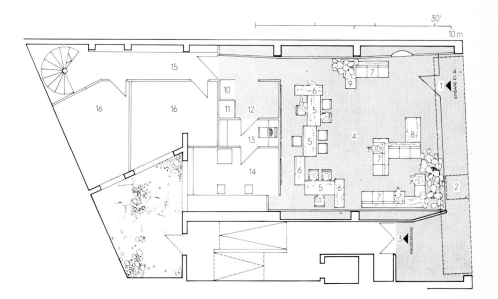

Greek Tourist Office and Gallery in Rome

Architect: Aris Konstantinidis, Athens

The Greek National Tourist Organization opened an information centre, part of which can also be used for exhibitions, in an old shop not far from the Via Veneto. By turning part of the floor above into a gallery and by converting a cellar, sufficient space was found in spite of the limited floor area. Each separate function of the office has a different floor level ascribed to it. A spiral staircase leads from the entrance to the manager's office on the gallery. The main space which houses the display area and the information desk is three steps higher than the entrance area. Next to the information desk, a staircase leads down into the cellar. Large windows and an all-glass door allow an unimpeded view from the street into the entrance area and the main room, which, as a result, becomes a display window with its walls decorated with photomontages and posters.

Griechisches Verkehrsbüro und Ausstellungs-raum in Rom

Architekt: Aris Konstantinidis, Athen

In einem alten Ladenlokal unweit der Via Veneto richtete die »Griechische Zentrale für Fremden-verkehr« ein Informationszentrum ein, das zugleich als Ausstellungsraum verwendet wird. Durch das Einziehen eines Galeriegeschosses und den Ausbau des Kellers war es möglich, trotz der be-engten Raumverhältnisse ausreichende Nutzfläche zu schaffen, wobei die einzelnen Bereiche nach Funktionen getrennt auf vier verschiedene Ebenen verteilt wurden. Vom Eingangsraum führt eine geschwungene Treppe zum Galeriegeschoß mit dem Arbeitsraum des Direktors hinauf. Der Haupt-raum mit Ausstellungszone und Auskunftstheke liegt drei Stufen höher als der Eingangsbereich. Neben dem Informationstisch führt eine Treppe zum Keller hinunter. Durch große Fensterflächen und die Ganzglastür sind Eingangs- und Hauptraum von der Straße aus voll einzusehen.

1. At night the information centre looks even more like a display window.

2–4. Plans and sections of the ground floor and the gallery. Plans. Key: 1 Entrance area, 2 Staircase to the gallery, 3 Display, 4 Information, 5 Seats, 6 Staircase to the cellar, 7 Gallery with manager's office and booking-office, 8 Airspace above the exhibition room, 9 Cellar and semi-basement.

5–7. Details of the display area. Floor of grey marble, ceiling and walls either white or covered with photomontages and posters. The wall beside the information desk is covered with terracotta tiles. A screen made of reed and coloured beads hangs in front of the staircase to the cellar.

1. Bei Nacht wird der »Schaufenster«-Charakter des Informationszentrums besonders deutlich.

2–4. Grundrisse von Erdgeschoß und Galeriegeschoß und Schnitt. Legende: 1 Eingangsraum, 2 Treppe zum Galeriegeschoß, 3 Ausstellung, 4 Auskunft, 5 Sitzgruppe, 6 Treppe zum Keller, 7 Galerie mit Direktion und Sekretariat, 8 Luftraum über dem Ausstellungsraum, 9 Keller mit Zwischengeschoß.

5–7. Detailansichten des Ausstellungsraums. Boden grauer Marmor, Decke und Wände weiß oder mit Photomontagen und Plakaten. Neben der Auskunftstheke Wand aus Terrakottaziegeln und vor der Treppe zum Keller Vorhang aus Schilfrohr mit farbigen Holzkugeln.

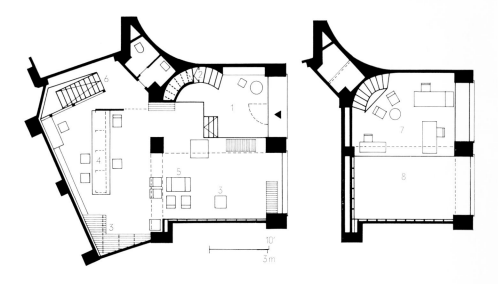

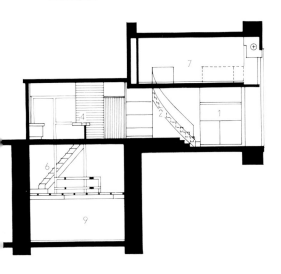

Index of Architects

Verzeichnis der Architekten

Photo Credits · Photonachweis